the artful bird

feathered FRIENDS
to make + SEW

abigail patner
glassenberg

INTERWEAVE
interweave.com

acknowledgments

SEWING BIRDS is pure joy for me! It is how I relax, think about what is going on in my life, and rejuvenate. I am thrilled to be able to turn this love into a book. I want to thank Tricia Waddell, editorial director at Interweave, for calling me half an hour after I e-mailed her my proposal, causing me to fall off my chair in disbelief. Tricia's excitement about my work, and her ability to help me refine my idea, showed me what a fine publisher Interweave truly is. Thank you to my editor, Elaine Lipson. Thanks also to Hilly Forsythe for being my pattern tester, and to my mother-in-law, Judi Glassenberg, for coming up with the book title.

My husband, Charlie, recognized early in our relationship that I need to be creative to stay happy. He has helped me to find time and space to create every day, even when family life became very busy. We were out on a rainy date night in April 2009, when I turned to him and said I had an idea for a craft book. Charlie's love, support, and keen editing ability kept me going as the process unfolded. His help and partnership helped me to focus on the big picture and the nitty-gritty and kept me laughing every step of the way. The births of my daughters, Roxanne and Stella, and my decision to stay at home with them, launched this hobby-turned-second career. I love their confidence that Mommy can make anything!

My parents, Bruce and Myra Patner, provided a creative household for my sister, Rachel, my brother, Matt, and me, when we were growing up. Crayons and Play-Doh and art lessons abounded. We were encouraged to come up with our own projects and we were allowed to play freely with high-quality materials. Art became part of my everyday life even as a young child, and I hope to provide that kind of environment for my own children.

And finally, thank you to all of my blog readers throughout the five years that I have written *whileshenaps*. My interactions with the online art and craft community keep me motivated and continue to inspire me every day.

EDITOR
Elaine Lipson
TECHNICAL EDITOR
Katrina Loving
ART DIRECTOR
Liz Quan
COVER + INTERIOR DESIGN
Pamela Norman
PHOTOGRAPHY
Brad Bartholomew
HOW-TO PHOTOGRAPHY
Joe Coca
PHOTO STYLIST
Ann Sabin Swanson
ILLUSTRATOR
Ann Sabin Swanson
PRODUCTION
Katherine Jackson

Interweave Press LLC
201 East Fourth Street
Loveland, CO 80537
interweave.com

Printed in China by Asia Pacific Offset Ltd.

Library of Congress Cataloging-
in-Publication Data

Glassenberg, Abigail Patner.
The artful bird : feathered friends to
make and sew / Abigail Patner Glassenberg.
p. cm.
Includes bibliographical references and index.
ISBN 978-1-59668-481-2 (eBook)
ISBN 978-1-59668-238-2 (pbk.)
1. Soft toy making. 2. Textile crafts.
3. Stuffed animals (Toys) 4. Birds in art.
I. Title.
TT174.3.G584 2010 745.592'4--dc22
2010028511

10 9 8 7 6 5 4 3 2 1

contents

birds are a magical subject...

...for artists and crafters. There are hundreds of varieties of birds, with endless variation in colors and feathers, size of beaks and length of toes, and shapes of heads and tails. People seem irresistibly drawn to the tiny size of birds, the look of wonderment in their eyes, their quick movements and, of course, their ability to fly.

MY BIRDMAKING JOURNEY began when I had my first child and took maternity leave from my job as a teacher, and then decided to stay home full time. I had enjoyed my job as a middle school teacher; I knew I was doing good work, but it was hard work. Being home with a baby was a different sort of hard work. I yearned to use my creative energy, so I began to sew.

I have always been a maker and have explored all kinds of art and crafts, from watercolors to origami, but sewing was always a constant and something I wanted to return to. I began to explore soft toy making in earnest. I searched my local library for books on sewing soft toys and found that most were published in the 1960s and 1970s, but were still informative; through them, I began to learn how soft toys were designed and sewn. I launched a blog (whileshenaps.typepad.com) to record my experiments, and I started to participate in the online craft community, where I learned about Japanese craft books. Despite the language barrier, I sewed up many soft toys from these books, too.

FROM MAKER TO DESIGNER

Through many hours of working with other people's patterns, I gained the skills and confidence to design my own toys. I always began with a sketch, worked with different elements I had been introduced to—gussets, darts, and underbodies—and developed designs that I loved. I began to sell my work at local craft shows and online and was invited to do a solo show at my library. For that exhibition, I made more than fifty designs, including my first birds. When the show was over, I knew I wanted to keep going with birds. For the next three years, I sewed birds almost exclusively.

I was no longer creating toys; each bird took several hours to complete and some were made with delicate vintage fabrics. To me, these fabric birds are really decorative objects for the home. Beautiful and evocative standing on a mantle or bookshelf, in the nursery, or in an office, each bird is one of a kind and very special. A fabric bird is like a little soul peering out in wonder, keeping you company.

HOW TO USE THIS BOOK

In this book, you'll find sixteen of my fabric bird patterns, as well as comprehensive sections on tools, materials, and basic birdmaking techniques that you can use to make any bird. I've included tips and tricks throughout for embellishing birds and using them in assemblages. I've also included interviews with four extraordinary fabric-bird artists for added inspiration and a gallery of their creations.

The materials I use to create fabric birds are readily available in most fabric stores. You probably already have most of them, and the few specialized tools I encourage you to invest in will most certainly be useful in tasks beyond birdmaking. A sewing machine, a few yards of colorful quilting cotton, thread, some wool or polyester stuffing, and wire from the hardware store, along with a pair of long tweezers or forceps, will get you started. I know you'll enjoy selecting fabrics and color combinations and enhancing each bird to make it your own.

Once you've sewn a few of the birds from this book, I encourage to you design your own patterns for birds. Nearly all of the birds are designed around the same three elements—underbody, side body, and head gusset. By playing with the shape and size of each of these basic elements you will be able to design your own bird. Delve into fabric birdmaking. I think once you see your first bird come to life you will share my excitement and want to make fabric birds of every variety. ~abby

materials + tools

These are the materials and tools you'll need to make the birds in this book. See project instructions for additional requirements for specific birds. In this chapter, I'll explain how I use these materials and tools in detail.

materials

- ☐ Tightly woven cotton fabrics, 45" (114.5 cm) wide, such as those used by quilters (I use plain fabrics for bird bodies and colored fabrics and prints for feathers and details)
- ☐ Wool stuffing (polyester stuffing may be substituted)
- ☐ Lightweight fusible interfacing
- ☐ Heavyweight interfacing, fusible on both sides, for flying birds (such as Fast2Fuse Heavyweight brand)
- ☐ Cotton batting
- ☐ Fusible web
- ☐ 16-gauge brass wire for legs and feet (or gauge indicated in pattern)
- ☐ Thread for hand and machine sewing
- ☐ Embroidery floss
- ☐ Floral tape
- ☐ Mixed-media embellishment and collage materials, such as beads, glitter, sequins, polymer clay, decorative papers, vintage and found fabrics, lace, and felt.

tools

- ☐ Freezer paper
- ☐ Sewing machine with walking foot
- ☐ Iron
- ☐ Scissors for paper and fabric
- ☐ Small embroidery scissors
- ☐ Pins (I use both regular straight pins and smaller appliqué pins)
- ☐ Sewing machine needles, size 11/75 or 12/80
- ☐ Handsewing needles
- ☐ Beeswax (to keep thread from tangling)
- ☐ Seam ripper
- ☐ Disappearing fabric marker (water or air soluble)
- ☐ Forceps or long craft tweezers
- ☐ Combination wire cutters/needle-nose pliers
- ☐ Spray-on fabric adhesive
- ☐ Craft glue
- ☐ E6000 glue
- ☐ Acrylic paints
- ☐ Acrylic sealer such as Mod Podge

fabric + stuffing

Good-quality base fabrics and stuffing materials are important to birdmaking success. Although the requirements for bird body fabrics are quite specific, you can indulge yourself when it comes to choosing fabric for feathers and embellishments—that's when anything goes. Before choosing fabrics for feathers, I look at the bird from a few feet away, or take a break and come back to it, having spent some time thinking about who this bird is and what I want it to look like in the end.

FABRIC

I experimented for years to discover the best fabrics for birdmaking. The fabric should be woven; it cannot have any stretch, or the finished bird will not hold its shape. The fabric must be thin enough to turn small pieces right side out properly, but not so thin that it will tear around the seams once the bird is stuffed.

The best fabric for bird bodies is high-quality quilting cotton. Vintage cottons are fine, as long as they are strong and tightly woven. I usually choose a solid or nearly solid color for the body, adding color with the wings and tail. For most birds, I use a light-colored fabric for the head so that beaded or embroidered eyes will show up well. Always prewash and dry all of your fabrics before you begin to cut and sew.

For the feathers that embellish a bird's wings and tail, I choose at least three fabrics in different values to give the wings some depth. These fabrics do not necessarily have to be quilting cotton, but if you plan to use torn strips to make looped feathers, most cotton fabrics tear easily. Select prints, hand-dyed fabrics, batiks, lace, vintage fabrics, or anything else that strikes you as beautiful. Hold colors up to each other and up to the bird, to try to imagine how they will look together. Use some of these fabrics for the other details the bird will need, such as eyes, an eye mask, or in the case of owls, ears. To make a more realistic bird, look through a birding guide to study the color combinations on the feathers of different species of birds before choosing fabric colors.

All of the fabric yardages given in the pattern instructions refer to fabric that is 45" (114.5 cm) wide. You'll often be able to use scraps of fabric; if you buy new yardage, you'll find that you often have fabric left over to save for the next project. Fabric and quilting stores also sell fabric in precut "fat quarters," a crosswise-cut ¼-yard piece that measures 18" x 22" (45.5 x 56 cm); these are a great way to build your fabric stash.

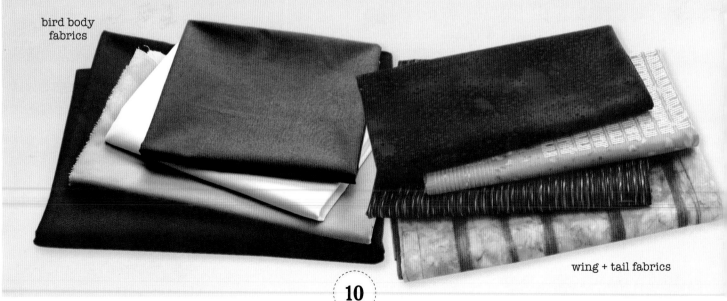

bird body fabrics

wing + tail fabrics

STUFFING

I use wool stuffing for birds. I like the feel of the natural fiber in my hands, and I find that wool stuffs very firmly. Unfortunately, wool stuffing is not widely available at craft and sewing stores, but you can find it online. I buy mine by the pound from an Amish farm in Pennsylvania and have it shipped to me. It is not much more expensive than polyester fiberfill and so much nicer to work with. If wool is not available to you, polyester fiberfill, sold at any craft, hobby, or fabric store, will work just fine for birdmaking.

tools for patternmaking + sewing

The items in this section are the basics of your sewing tool kit. Freezer paper, my favorite patternmaking material, is sold at grocery stores everywhere, and all of the sewing tools are easy to find on the notions wall of your local sewing or craft store.

FREEZER PAPER

Freezer paper is essential to my birdmaking process. It is available by the roll in the grocery store, near the wax paper and foil. It's inexpensive and wonderful for making sewing patterns. Freezer paper will temporarily adhere to fabric when placed shiny side down and pressed with a warm iron. Freezer paper is translucent enough to trace patterns directly onto it and allows for accuracy when working with small parts, such as a bird beak. See Basic Birdmaking Techniques, page 19, for detailed instructions on my method of making and using freezer paper patterns.

INTERFACING

Interfacing is a material used to give structure to garments and sewn objects. It can be woven or nonwoven, fusible (made to adhere to fabric when pressed with an iron) or sew-in, and comes in a variety of weights. I use both heavyweight and lightweight nonwoven fusible interfacing when constructing wings and tails for the birds; it's a good idea to have some of each on hand.

Interfacing is sold by the yard or in packages; it's usually white, but some brands are also available in black.

In smaller birds, the tails benefit from a layer or two of lightweight interfacing, so that they don't droop under the weight of the feathers made from torn strips or punched shapes. I usually use a fusible interfacing for this, sandwiching it between the two pieces of fabric I've cut for the tail, pressing to fuse, and then ironing down the freezer-paper pattern pieces that I will stitch around.

For birds designed to be in flight, I use the heaviest fusible interfacing available. This material feels almost like thick cardboard and holds its shape very well.

BATTING

Batting is fiber sold in sheets for quilting and crafts; it's available in cotton, polyester, or blends of the two (silk and wool battings are sold, but are not as widely available). I use cotton batting when I make quilted wings and tails for my birds. This is the simplest method

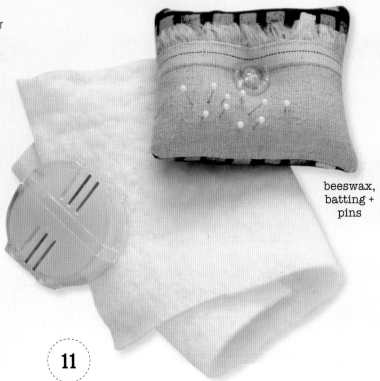

beeswax, batting + pins

of making these parts. Cotton batting is a soft, natural fiber that's easy to work with, and it's readily available at fabric and craft stores. If you buy a small package, such as a batting intended for a crib quilt, you'll be able to make quite a few wings and tails with it.

FUSIBLE WEB

Fusible web is an adhesive material that is activated with the heat of an iron. Fusible web is double-sided, so it can connect both a top and a bottom layer of fabric, and comes in varying weights. I use lightweight web for adhering fabrics that will be punched or cut into feathers.

SEWING MACHINE WITH WALKING FOOT

It's necessary to sew the bodies of bird sculptures by machine so that the stitching is small and strong enough to stand up to the stress of firm stuffing. A basic sewing machine with a standard presser foot for straight stitch and the capacity to backstitch is sufficient. I use a special presser foot attachment called a walking foot to sew my birds. Traditionally used for quilting or sewing tricky fabrics such as velvet, it makes it easier to sew small bird parts. The walking foot helps the layers of fabric feed evenly through the machine.

THREAD

Any polyester or cotton-covered polyester all-purpose thread can be used for creating birds. I often choose a contrasting thread color when I sew a bird because I like to see the stitches along the seam line. To me, the evidence of the maker's hand adds interest to the finished bird. If you prefer a more subtle look, choose a thread that matches the body color.

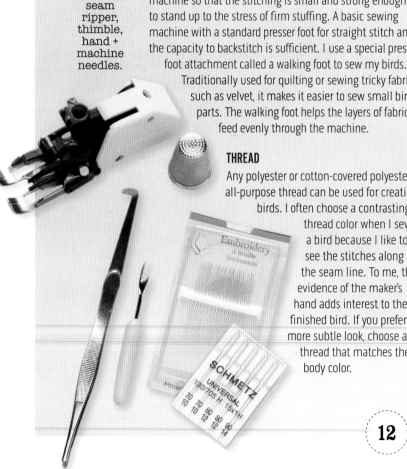

walking foot, craft tweezers, seam ripper, thimble, hand + machine needles.

HANDSEWING NEEDLES

For handsewing, I use size 8 crewel or embroidery needles. These are thin, sharp needles that allow for easy maneuvering when sewing small parts, yet have an eye large enough for easy threading. The larger eye means I can use the same needle for embroidering details on the birds. I always have at least a half-dozen fresh embroidery needles in my needle book, ready for when I need them.

MACHINE-SEWING NEEDLES

I use a size 11/75 or 12/80 sewing machine needle when stitching birds. Machine needles vary in size from the heaviest weight needle, a 19/120, used for sewing uphol-stery-weight fabrics, to the lightest, an 8/60, for sheer fabrics. The birds in this book are all sewn from tightly woven quilting cotton, and they are stuffed very firmly. It is important that the needle not be too large or it will create holes in the fabric when the bird is stuffed that will weaken the seams. When you begin a bird, be sure to use a fresh needle. Dull needles have the tendency to push small pattern pieces down into the machine.

PINS

I use sharp glass-head straight pins when I sew. These pins will neither damage the fabric nor leave a big hole when removed, and glass heads will not melt if they accidentally end up under an iron.

When I am sewing beaks or attaching small parts, I use small appliqué pins. These pins are about half the size of standard pins, and they don't get in the way when sewing small parts by hand. I keep a pincushion near my machine, another on the cutting board, and a third on the ironing board. You can never have too many pincushions, and they are fun to make!

BEESWAX

When sewing by hand, keep a circle of beeswax, available at craft and fabric stores, nearby; run the thread through the beeswax once or twice before stitching. The beeswax coating strengthens the thread and helps keep it from tangling.

SEAM RIPPER

I sew my birds with a very small stitch length—about 16 stitches to 1" (2.5 cm), which corresponds to the No. 2 marking on the dial of my sewing machine. Mistakes are an inevitable part of sewing, though, and there will be times when you accidentally sew a seam upside down or backward; when that happens, all those tiny stitches so close together can be time-consuming to unpick. Use a small seam ripper tool; I keep mine next to my machine, and it makes unpicking fast and painless, so that I can get on with my creative work.

DISAPPEARING INK FABRIC MARKER

You'll find many different kinds of tools for marking fabric available at any fabric or craft store. For drawing in eyes and other markings before stitching, I like to use a water-soluble ink fabric marker that's designed to disappear when sprayed with water; I keep a spray bottle handy in my studio and mist any exposed marks after stitching and before pressing. Air-soluble ink markers are also available, designed to evaporate after exposure to air for a few days.

scissors + forceps

Never skimp on scissors that you'll use for cutting fabric. They should have a sharp edge and be comfortable to hold and use. Forceps are, perhaps, the most unusual tool in my bird-making arsenal. I find that they work better than anything else I've tried for maneuvering small pieces of bird bodies!

SCISSORS

I use three pairs of scissors when I make a bird. The first is a pair that I keep just for cutting paper. I use these to cut out pattern pieces from freezer paper. The second is a pair of sharp dressmaker's shears meant for cutting fabric. I use these when I am cutting around larger pattern pieces and for cutting interfacing or batting down to size. Finally, I have a pair of small, sharp sewing scissors (or embroidery shears). I use these small scissors the most, because the pattern pieces I work with are all rela-

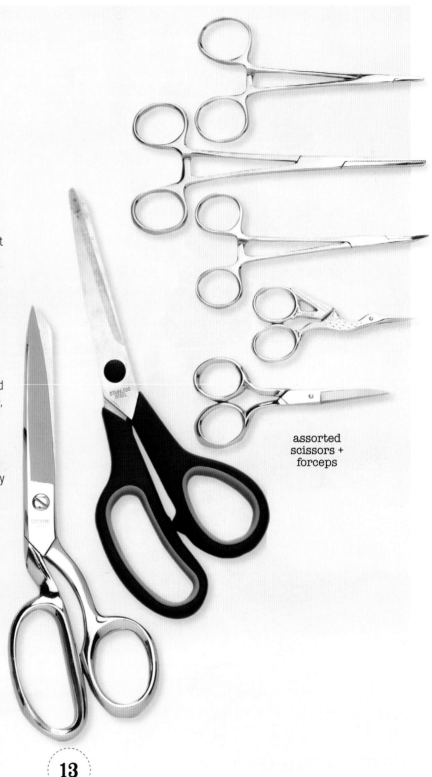

assorted
scissors +
forceps

tively small, and they allow me to cut accurately around the curves and angles. They're also useful for snipping threads.

FORCEPS

Surgical forceps, also called hemostats, are my most important birdmaking tool. I use forceps for turning bird bodies right side out and for stuffing them. Forceps have handles and blades like scissors, but the points are dull, not sharp, and are designed for grasping small items. If you do not have a pair of forceps and plan to sew more than a few soft sculptures, invest in a pair. You'll find them on websites that sell supplies for making teddy bears. I got mine for free from an eye surgeon, so you might even try your local hospital, too; forceps come in suture kits and are often unused and discarded.

Using forceps will dramatically reduce your frustration when turning small bird parts, such as beaks, right side out, and when stuffing them. The small tip can reach easily into spaces that are much too tiny for fingers. My favorite pair of forceps has little ridges on the inside of the clamp. These ridges give a little traction when pinching tiny bits of fabric, such as the tip of a beak or the base of a leg. Long craft tweezers can also be used for turning and stuffing, and they're readily available at fabric and craft stores. I prefer to use forceps, but everyone's hands are

floral tape,
wire cutters +
spools of wire

different, and you may find that tweezers fit your hands better. Whichever you choose, remember to be gentle when turning and stuffing, to avoid piercing a hole in the fabric with your tool.

supplies for building bird legs

Although you may have sewing supplies already on hand, these materials and tools might require a trip to the craft store and hardware store. Bird legs and feet give the bird personality, and of course, they'll help your three-dimensional creation stand and balance, so it's important to spend some time on these details.

WIRE

Wire is best purchased at the hardware store. Look in the picture framing section for wire sold in rolls. I prefer 16-gauge brass wire for birds because it is strong enough to create stable legs and feet, while still malleable enough to bend with a simple pair of pliers. For smaller birds, 18-gauge wire works. I do not recommend copper wire or any wire with a gauge higher than 18 because it bends too easily and will not be strong enough to support the weight of the bird.

WIRE CUTTERS

It's also easiest to buy wire cutters at the hardware store instead of the craft or fabric store. Look for a pair of wire cutters that also functions as needle-nose pliers. This tool is lightweight, sharp, and effective, and it's the best tool for forming the wire legs and feet on the birds in this book.

FLORAL TAPE

I searched for a long time to find a way to cover and color the wire legs on the birds while still maintaining their very thin profile. Floral tape was the answer! Almost all of the birds in this book have wire legs that are wrapped with floral tape, and it's a wonderful product to work with.

Floral tape has stretch to it, allowing you to wrap the wire very tightly. Floral tape is not sticky. The wax coating on the tape warms in your hands and begins to melt a bit as you work with it, fusing the layers of tape together. With a bit of practice on scrap lengths of wire, you will be able to wrap wire tightly and smoothly.

Floral tape is inexpensive and readily available at craft stores in the flower arranging section. I have also bought it from my local florist. Although you'll most often see green tape, florists frequently have more unusual colors, such as brown and black, and will sell you a roll at a very fair price—just ask! If you can't find the color you're looking for, simply use what you have and paint it any color with acrylic paint after wrapping the bird's legs.

adhesives + sealer

Adhesives and acrylic sealer are helpful at various stages of birdmaking. These are the products I use in my studio for either temporary or permanent bonds or to seal painted legs or beaks. Always follow safety precautions when using adhesives; use in a well-ventilated area, protect your skin and eyes from contact, and observe any and all warning labels on the package.

SPRAY ADHESIVE

Spray adhesive is handy for placing eyes and punched feathers before sewing. Always be sure to work in a well-ventilated area and wear a dust mask if recommended on the container. Work on newspaper or other protective surface.

CRAFT GLUE

Basic all-purpose white craft glue that dries clear is useful on many birdmaking projects and should be in your tool kit.

E6000 CRAFT GLUE

I use E6000, a strong craft glue, for adhering polymer clay beaks to birds. This glue is available in craft stores.

TWO-PART EPOXY

Two-part epoxy is good for constructing mixed-media backdrops for birds. I like epoxy with a long drying time because it gives the strongest hold. I use it often when I want to attach a bird securely to a perch or another object in an assemblage, mixing and applying with a popsicle stick. Epoxy glues are toxic, so follow all safety precautions very carefully; use gloves, safety goggles or glasses, and work in a well-ventilated area. Store epoxy products out of reach of children and pets.

ACRYLIC SEALER

An acrylic sealer, such as Mod Podge, is wonderful for découpaging bits of paper ephemera to a backdrop, such as a small stretched canvas or a wooden box, that will hold a bird. Use a small craft brush; do not use any water on your brush, just dip the brush into the sealer and apply sealer to the support. Press the paper down onto the wet sealer and smooth out any air bubbles with your fingers, then apply a coat of sealer on top of the paper. You can also use acrylic sealer to finish a bird's legs and feet for a smooth, finished look after you've wrapped them with floral tape and painted with acrylic paint.

adhesives, acrylic paints + sealer

six-strand
embroidery floss
in neutral colors
for eyes, embroi-
dery needles,
thimble + stitched
eye piece.

supplies for embroidering + embellishing

The personality of a bird is in the details, and this is where the mixed-media crafter in you can have some fun. Embroider eyes, add beads, use glitter, and even create beaks with polymer clay to add color, sparkle, and expression to your creation.

EMBROIDERY FLOSS

Embroidery floss is ideal for embroidering eyes on birds; it comes in every color imaginable, but I choose neutrals to embroider bird eyes, including browns, tans, black, and creams. Choose brighter colors for a more whimsical look. Floss is made of six strands of cotton or rayon; gently pull two strands from a cut length and thread a needle with both strands. Working with two strands allows you to create fine detail while filling in a larger space efficiently.

BEADS

Keep a supply of perfectly round black beads, a bit larger than seed beads, for making eyes for birds. Bead eyes are quick to sew, and they create an endearing expression on a bird. Use beads to embellish wings and tails. For embellishment, use any pretty beads, including seed beads and pearls. Sew the beads firmly to a wing base and then tack the wing to the bird in the usual manner.

GLITTER

Glitter is an easy-to-apply embellishment for bird wings and tails. Choose a glitter that closely matches the color of the fabric that it will adhere to so that it does not stand out too much, but just adds sparkle. Glitter looks festive, and I most often use glitter when making a bird that will be part of a holiday decoration. To apply glitter, spray the fabric with spray adhesive. Shake the glitter liberally over the tacky area and allow the adhesive to dry completely. Shake any excess glitter over a trash can. Sew glittered wings and tail to a bird body in the regular fashion.

POLYMER CLAY

I use polymer clay to create beaks for some birds. Small squares of polymer clay are readily available at most craft and hobby stores for a few dollars. Shape the soft clay and then bake in a conventional oven according to package instructions to harden the form. It only takes a pinch of clay for a beak, so one square of clay will be enough for at least six birds. Polymer clay is very malleable and comes in a rainbow of colors. After baking a clay beak, sand the piece if fingerprints are visible. If you like, paint the beak with acrylic paints or seal with an acrylic sealer. Use a dab of strong craft glue, such as E6000, to adhere the baked clay beak to the bird.

ACRYLIC PAINTS

If you cannot find the color of floral tape that you want for making bird legs and feet, or if you want to add extra shading to the legs and feet of a bird, paint the wrapped legs and feet of a bird with acrylic paints. Whether painted or unpainted, the legs and feet can also be sealed with an acrylic sealer, such as Mod Podge, to give them a smooth, finished look.

glitter for embellishing wings + polymer clay

basic birdmaking techniques

Here you'll find detailed instructions for the processes that I use to make birds, and you'll learn techniques that are common to all the birds in this book. When you've mastered these methods, you'll have a foundation for making all of the patterns that follow or for designing and creating your own original birds.

general instructions

Read through these instructions carefully before you begin, even if you have sewing experience. Some techniques, such as placing patterns at random instead of on a specific grain direction, are unique to my method of birdmaking.

SEAM ALLOWANCES

All seams are stitched with a ¼" (6 mm) seam allowance unless otherwise specified. The seam allowance is not included in the patterns; add a ¼" (6 mm) seam allowance to the main body pieces (side body, underbody, gussets) for all patterns. To create a ¼" (6 mm) seam allowance, iron the freezer paper pattern pieces to the fabric. Cut the fabric ¼" (6 mm) outside of the edge of the pattern piece. Sew the pieces together ¼" (6 mm) from the edge of the fabric.

Wings and tails do not require adding a seam allowance. Simply iron the freezer paper pattern pieces to the fabric and sew directly around them with the pattern still adhered to the fabric. Then pull off the pattern piece and trim ⅛" (3 mm) around the stitching line. The fabric beaks and other small parts are also sewn this way because a ¼" (6 mm) seam allowance is too wide for such tiny pattern pieces.

GRAIN DIRECTION

With traditional sewing patterns, it's important to pay careful attention to the grain of the fabric when placing pattern pieces. When sewing birds, I've found it's more interesting to ignore the grain direction of the fabric. Each bird reveals its personality this way.

Sometimes I cut one side body pattern piece with the grain direction running horizontally and then purposely turn the fabric and cut the second side body on the diagonal, or with the grain direction running vertically. When the bird is stuffed the neck will arch and turn, giving the bird a quizzical and endearing personality. Ignoring grain direction also allows me to use very tiny scraps of fabric. No piece goes to waste, and my tiniest, treasured scraps become a head gusset or a beak. If you prefer a more predictable process, cut all pattern pieces with the grain.

MACHINE STITCH LENGTH

When sewing sculptures from quilting cotton, you must use a very small stitch length. The stitches need to be tight and close together, so that when the body is stuffed, the seams will not burst. I stuff my birds very firmly, packing the stuffing as tightly as possible. This is especially important when making birds that stand on a wire armature, because shifting or compacting of the stuffing can cause space to form around the wire, making the legs loosen inside, and the bird will be off balance. On my machine, a stitch length setting of No. 2 on the dial works best for me; this is about 16 stitches to 1" (2.5 cm). Backstitch at the start and end of all seams unless otherwise stated.

BASTING

Basting by hand is a great trick for keeping edges neat. Basting holds an edge in place more firmly than pins do and keeps it in place while you stuff, without pins getting in the way.

To baste a raw edge by hand, neatly fold it inward and iron it flat. Thread a needle with a double length of thread, but do not knot the end. Use a long,

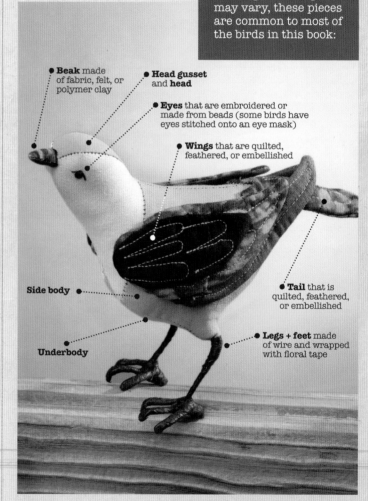

THE ANATOMY OF A BIRD

Although the shapes may vary, these pieces are common to most of the birds in this book:

Beak made of fabric, felt, or polymer clay

Head gusset and **head**

Eyes that are embroidered or made from beads (some birds have eyes stitched onto an eye mask)

Wings that are quilted, feathered, or embellished

Tail that is quilted, feathered, or embellished

Side body

Underbody

Legs + feet made of wire and wrapped with floral tape

loose running stitch along the folded edge. After stuffing, pull out the basting stitches. Basting is especially useful for sewing beaks neatly.

EMBROIDERY STITCHES

See the stitch glossary, page 137, for diagrams of simple embroidery stitches that you'll need to embroider eye details.

bird construction

This section covers tracing and cutting patterns from freezer paper and constructing, turning, and stuffing the bird body.

1 TRACE + CUT PATTERNS

Trace the pattern pieces in this book directly onto the matte side of freezer paper with a pencil **(fig. 1a)**. Alternatively, cut a sheet of freezer paper to a size that will go through your printer, scan the pattern, and print it directly onto the matte side of the freezer paper.

Cut out the pattern piece with scissors designated for paper. Press the glossy side of the pattern piece to a piece of fabric with a warm iron to secure it temporarily **(fig. 1b)**. You can then cut around the shape ¼" (6 mm) away from the pattern piece and then pull the pattern piece off before sewing the fabric. In some cases, such as when stitching a beak or a crest, you'll be instructed to machine stitch directly around the

pattern piece while it is still attached to the fabric. I use both techniques in creating birds.

Be sure to label each pattern piece with the type of bird, the name of the pattern piece, how many pieces of fabric you'll need to cut with it, and any markings, such as darts or notches. Once you are finished with the pattern, collect all the pattern pieces in an envelope to use again. Freezer paper patterns can be ironed onto and removed from fabric up to a dozen times before they'll no longer adhere successfully. When that happens, simply redraw them on fresh freezer paper.

2 CUT BIRD BODY PIECES FROM FABRIC

Unless the pattern directs otherwise, use these general instructions for cutting bird body pieces. Remember

that for the Side Body and Underbody pieces of each bird, you'll need a right and left version of each piece, as they are asymmetrical. You can do this by folding the fabric and cutting both pieces at once or by cutting one pattern piece, flipping the fabric over, re-ironing the pattern piece and cutting again. To cut out both side body pieces at once, fold fabric in half, right sides together. Place the side body pattern piece on the fabric, matte side up, and iron it down using the cotton setting on your iron, as shown in **fig. 1b**.

Cut around the pattern piece, adding a ¼" (6 mm) seam allowance all the way around. You can eyeball this or draw the seam allowance ¼" (6 mm) outside the pattern piece with a light pencil or disappearing ink fabric marker before cutting.

Transfer all pattern markings onto the fabric with a disappearing ink fabric marker.

Repeat the same process for cutting the underbody pieces, transferring the markings for the darts, when applicable. Cut the head gusset and any other gussets from a single layer of fabric **(fig. 2a)**.

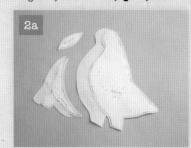

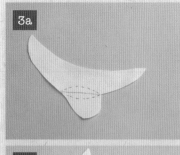

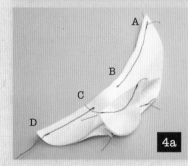

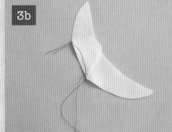

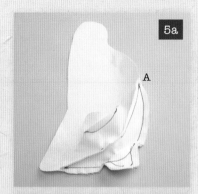

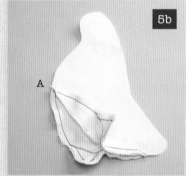

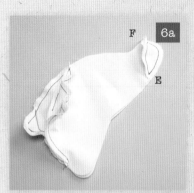

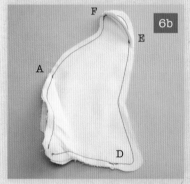

3 SEW UNDERBODY DARTS

Begin by sewing up the darts on an underbody piece **(fig. 3a)**.

Fold the bottom of the leg of one underbody upward along the straight line and press.

Machine stitch along the curved dotted line to create the dart **(fig. 3b)**.

Repeat on the other underbody.

Fold the darted legs down and pin to keep them out of the way.

4 ATTACH THE TWO UNDERBODIES

Place the underbodies on top of one another, right sides together, and pin across the top edges.

Beginning at point A, sew to point B. Leave a 1" (2.5 cm) opening for turning and stuffing as marked on the pattern piece. Sew from point C to point D **(fig. 4a)**.

5 SEW UNDERBODY TO THE SIDE BODIES

Open up the underbody. Align one side of it, right sides together, with one side body piece. Pin in place.

Sew from point A to the base of the leg, leaving a space at the base for inserting the leg wire later.

Sew from the base of the leg up to point D **(fig. 5a)**.

Repeat, sewing the other side body to the underbody.

Be sure to pay particular attention to lining up all the seams at point A because this will be the breast of the bird **(fig. 5b)**.

6 SEW THE HEAD GUSSET + BIRD BODY

Place the head gusset, right sides together, on one side body.

Sew from E to F.

Match up the other side body with

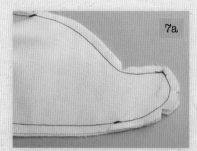

the head gusset and sew from E to F **(fig. 6a)**.

Now finish sewing around the entire bird from the breast, point A, to the tip of the head gusset, point F, and from the base of the tail, point D, to the end of the head gusset, point E **(fig. 6b)**.

7 REINFORCE SEAMS + CLIP CURVES

Examine the sewn bird carefully. If necessary, reinforce any weak seams with additional stitching by stitching them again just inside the seam line.

Clip the curves with either a small slit or a notch, especially at the head and the inner and outer thighs, being sure not to cross the stitching line **(fig. 7a)**.

Trim across the tail, just outside the stitching line, to reduce the extra fabric there.

8 TURN BODY RIGHT SIDE OUT

Turning the bird body right side out is an important step; take your time, be gentle, and work patiently! Always pull the extremities into the body first when turning a bird right side out.

With forceps or long craft tweez-

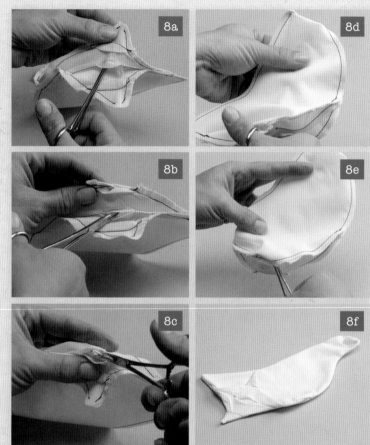

ers, reach into the bird through the opening between the underbodies **(fig. 8a)**. To turn, squeeze the handles of the forceps or tweezers together, clamping them shut, with fabric sandwiched between the tips **(fig. 8b)**.

Grasp the tip of one leg and pull it into the body **(fig. 8c)**. Pull the other leg into the body in the same way.

Grasp the head and pull it in **(fig. 8d)**, and then the tail **(fig. 8e)**.

Now, grasp the head again and pull it gently through the opening. Continue to gently pull the bird right side out, being careful not to pull too hard with forceps or tweezers, which could tear the fabric. I like to use my hands for this so I can make sure I am not tearing any seams.

Once the bird is turned, gently poke the extremities with forceps or tweezers to make sure they are fully turned **(fig. 8f)**.

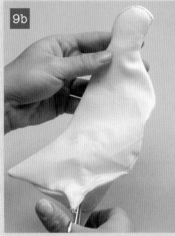

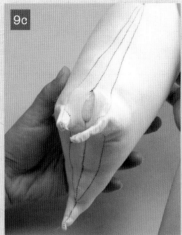

with the tips of your forceps. Then, insert the tip of the forceps into the body, going all the way to the extremity, and pack the stuffing into it as tightly as possible **(fig. 9a)**.

Begin by pushing the stuffing into the very top of the bird's head **(fig. 9b)**.

Continue grabbing small bits of stuffing and packing it tightly until the head is firmly stuffed, then work your way down. Continue stuffing almost the entire bird in this fashion **(fig. 9c)**.

Do not stuff the legs yet and leave a small space just above the legs that is not stuffed.

The stuffed bird should feel very firm and hard and should not be squishy at all. The process does not move quickly, and it really cannot be rushed, but it is worthwhile to stuff with care so that you end up with a smooth, firmly stuffed bird body.

9 STUFF THE BIRD

Stuffing is one of the most important steps in the creation of a bird. Stuffing properly takes time. I find that after cutting, sewing, and turning a bird, it is best to take a break before stuffing. Come back fresh so that you can devote all of your attention to stuffing slowly and carefully.

The birds in this book need to be stuffed very firmly. The best way to do this is to grab tiny bits of stuffing

10 INSERT THE LEG WIRE

Now you're starting to see a real bird come to life. The next step is adding the wire that will become the legs and feet. When you have about ½" (1.3 cm) of bird body remaining to be stuffed, pause to insert the wire as follows.

Use wire cutters to cut a length of wire for the legs. Larger birds will require about 48" (122 cm) of wire, smaller birds about 36" (91.5 cm).

Bend the wire in half, creating a long V **(fig. 10a)**.

Insert one tip of the V into the opening between the underbody pieces **(fig. 10b)**.

Thread it down through one leg and out the little opening at the base of the leg **(fig. 10c)**.

Pull the wire almost entirely out through this opening, continuing to pull past the halfway point until the other tip is visible through the opening between the underbody pieces **(fig. 10d)**.

Thread this tip into the other leg and out through the little opening at the base of the leg **(fig. 10e)**.

Now pull the tips of the wire until the bend at the halfway point is centered in the opening between the underbody pieces **(fig. 10f)**.

Push the bend into the stuffing to bury it as much as possible in the body.

Holding the wire in place with one hand, grasp some stuffing with forceps or tweezers with the other

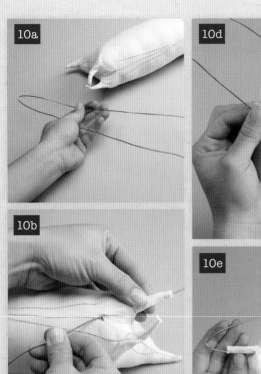

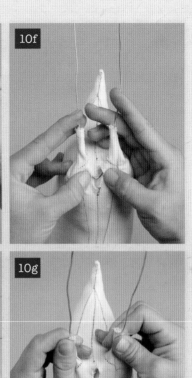

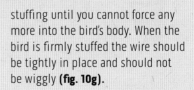

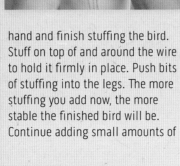

hand and finish stuffing the bird. Stuff on top of and around the wire to hold it firmly in place. Push bits of stuffing into the legs. The more stuffing you add now, the more stable the finished bird will be. Continue adding small amounts of stuffing until you cannot force any more into the bird's body. When the bird is firmly stuffed the wire should be tightly in place and should not be wiggly **(fig. 10g)**.

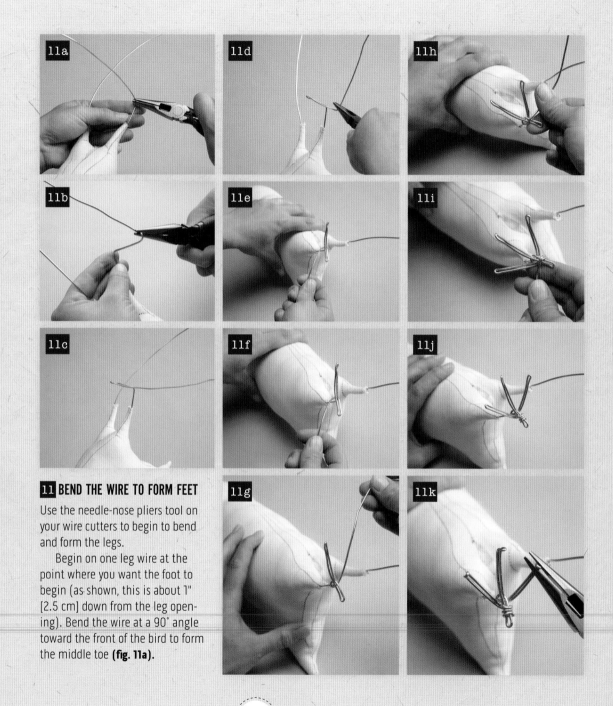

11 BEND THE WIRE TO FORM FEET

Use the needle-nose pliers tool on your wire cutters to begin to bend and form the legs.

Begin on one leg wire at the point where you want the foot to begin (as shown, this is about 1" [2.5 cm] down from the leg open-ing). Bend the wire at a 90˚ angle toward the front of the bird to form the middle toe **(fig. 11a)**.

Bend the wire back to finish the toe **(figs. 11b, 11c)**.

About ½" (1.3 cm) behind the leg, bend the wire back toward the front to form the back toe **(fig. 11d)**. The toes should be ½" to 1½" (1.3 to 3.8 cm) long, depending on the size of the bird.

Now wrap the wire tightly around the leg one time to add stability to the foot **(figs. 11e, 11f, 11g)**.

Bend the wire again to create an inner toe and then wrap it tightly around the back toe for added stability **(fig. 11h)**.

Bend the wire to create an outer toe and end by wrapping it a few times around the back toe **(fig. 11i)**.

Cut off the excess wire; make sure the cut end is pushed flush to the back toe, because it can be sharp **(fig. 11j)**. Use the tip of the pliers to squeeze the ends of each toe, closing them as much as possible.

Curve the end of each toe downward a bit, creating talons **(fig. 11k)**.

Repeat this process with the other leg, making sure the legs match in length and the toes match in length.

12 BALANCE THE BIRD

Bending the feet can cause the stuffing to compact inside the bird. Take a moment to add more stuffing so that the legs are as stable as possible. Now work on balancing the bird so that it stands on its own **(fig. 12a)**. Balancing takes patience. I find it helpful to stand the bird up and put one hand

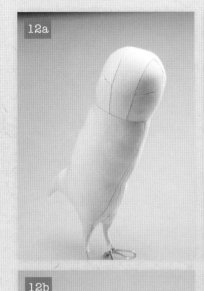

12a

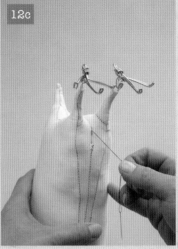

12c

12b

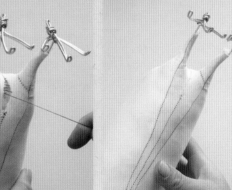

12d

firmly on the feet while moving the bird's body with the other hand.

You may need to use your pliers to bend some of the toes a bit more.

On some birds, I bend the legs forward to give the bird a more natural stance. Study images of birds in a birding book to see how they

naturally stand and try to mimic this stance with wire.

Once the bird is standing on its own, close the opening between the underbodies with neat handsewn ladder stitches **(figs. 12b, 12c, 12d)**. (*Ladder stitch is illustrated on page 137*).

13 WRAP THE LEGS + FEET WITH FLORAL TAPE

I wrap the legs of each of my birds with floral tape, which gives the legs a smooth, finished look, and lends some stability to the bird. For some of the larger birds, I wrap the legs a second time with torn strips of fabric and a third time with contrasting thread. This gives the legs some heft and texture.

Cut a 24" (61 cm) length of floral tape.

Place one end of the tape where the fabric and wire meet at the top of one leg. Holding the end of the tape there with one hand, begin to wrap the tape tightly around itself, covering where the fabric and wire meet, and then working your way down the leg (fig. 13a).

Pull and stretch the floral tape so that it wraps tightly. It will warm in your hands, and the waxy coating will fuse the tape to itself, forming a tight seal around the leg.

At the base of the leg, begin to wrap the toes (fig. 13b).

Be sure to wrap each toe completely so that no wire is showing (fig. 13c).

If you run out of floral tape, seal the end onto the leg, place the short end of the new length against the leg, hold it in place, and continue wrapping until the entire leg and foot are covered.

Repeat for the other leg (fig. 13d).

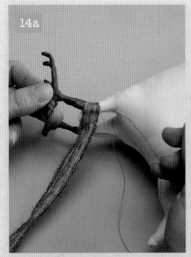

14a

14c

14e

14b

14d

14f

14 WRAP THE LEGS + FEET WITH FABRIC + THREAD

For larger birds, I overwrap the legs with torn fabric strips and thread to add visual interest and texture.

Tear a strip of fabric about ¼" (6 mm) wide and 24" (61 cm) long, and press it with your iron.

Lay one short end, wrong side up, on top of the floral tape where the floral tape meets the fabric at the top of the leg. Stitch it down by hand with a few stitches **(fig. 14a)**.

Flip the strip over to the right side and begin to firmly wrap the leg **(fig. 14b)**.

Wrap the fabric strip all the way down to the base of the leg and then

14g

14h

14j

14i

14k

around each toe, including the back toe (**figs. 14c, 14d**).

Leave the tips of each toe exposed because these will be the bird's talons (**fig. 14e**).

Finish wrapping the fabric, ending at the bottom of the foot, and pin it in place (**fig. 14f**). If the strip is too long, trim it.

Tuck the raw edge of the short end of the strip under and secure the strip to the bottom of the foot with a few stitches (**fig. 14g**). Repeat for the other leg (**fig. 14h**).

To add thread wrapping, thread a needle with a single 24" (61 cm) length of contrasting thread. Take one stitch at the top of the leg where the fabric strip begins. Tug on the knot, pulling it into the bird's body (**fig. 14i**).

Wrap the thread around the leg, working your way down, and then around each toe (**fig. 14j**). Continue wrapping back up the leg and take a single stitch at the top of the leg, tying a knot to secure the thread. Trim off any extra length of thread. Repeat for the other leg (**fig. 14k**).

Stand the bird up and make any adjustments so that it balances well.

wings + tail

I often wait until I have a turned, stuffed, standing bird before I decide what sort of wings it might have and what color scheme to use. To me, the wings are a blank canvas, and this is my opportunity to be creative with colors, textures, and materials. The simplest method is to make quilted wings and tail. Wings and tails with "feathers" take more time but also add complexity, texture, and visual interest. This section explores both techniques along with more ideas for creative wings and tails.

15 QUILTED WINGS + TAIL

The simplest way to create wings and tails is to sandwich batting between fabric layers and quilt to add dimension and visual interest. This is a fast, but still beautiful, way to make wings and tails. I like cotton batting best because it is so soft, but polyester batting will also work for these projects.

Cut a piece of batting roughly the shape of the wing or tail, but ¼" (6 mm) larger.

Cut two pieces of fabric this same size and place them right sides together. Put the fabric on top of the batting, creating a sandwich: batting on the bottom, then two layers of fabric, right sides together, on top. Iron the pattern piece on top of the sandwich **(fig. 15a)**.

Stitch around the pattern piece through all layers, leaving an opening of about 1" (2.5 cm) for turning

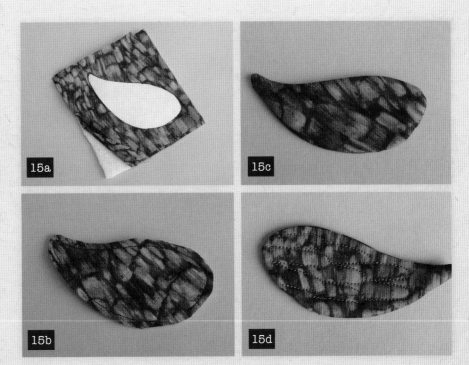

15a
15c
15b
15d

(fig. 15b). Pull off the pattern piece and trim the seam allowance around the stitching line to ⅛" (3 mm).

Insert forceps between the two fabric layers and grasp the furthest tip of the wing. Gently pull the wing right side out. Iron it flat and tuck in the raw edges of the opening, ironing them flat as well **(fig. 15c)**.

Stitch the opening closed with ladder stitch. Now, quilt the wing. I like to draw a feathery design with a disappearing ink fabric pen and stitch over it on the machine **(fig. 15d)**. Handquilting can give a beautiful effect, too.

16 BASE FOR WINGS + TAIL WITH FABRIC FEATHERS

The first step in creating a feathered wing is to sew up a wing base that will hold loops, punched shapes, or other feathery embellishments. The wing and tail bases can be any fabric color, because they will be covered later and will not show.

Cut two mirror-image wing patterns and one tail pattern from freezer paper.

Cut two pieces of fabric roughly the shape of a wing but ¼" (6 mm) larger. Place them wrong sides together. Iron one wing pattern piece on top **(fig. 16a)**.

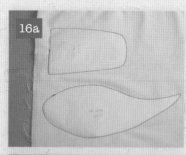

16a

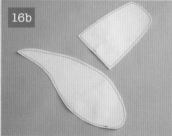

16b

Stitch alongside the edge of the freezer paper around the pattern piece through both layers. Remove freezer paper.

Cut out the shape through both fabric layers, cutting ⅛" (3 mm) from the stitching line **(fig. 16b)**.

Repeat for the other wing, using the second wing pattern that you've traced onto freezer paper.

Using the tail pattern piece, repeat for the tail.

Wing and tail bases that are to be embellished with fabric feathers have raw edges and are not turned.

17 BASE FOR WINGS + TAIL OF A BIRD IN FLIGHT

I love creating birds in flight, with wings that give the impression that the bird is soaring through the air, because this pose is so graceful.

To capture it, though, I had to find a way to stiffen the fabric wings enough that they would hold their shape, even under the weight of sewn feathers. Then I discovered heavy interfacing that is fusible on both sides and as sturdy as cardboard. The stiffness it provides is necessary to form wings that are stretched out in flight. This type of interfacing is available at craft and fabric stores; ask for the heaviest weight available.

To create the wing and tail base for flying birds, cut a piece of heavy-weight interfacing, fusible on both sides, that is roughly the shape of your wing pattern piece. Fuse it between the wrong sides of two layers of fabric that will become the wing. Each layer of fabric should have the right side facing out, because these wings are not turned.

Cut and sew the darts (marked on pattern templates for flying bird patterns). Iron the pattern piece to the fabric, then sew all the way around the wing.

After sewing, trim neatly around the shape, trimming ⅛" (3 mm) from the stitching line. You now have a stiff wing on which to sew torn strips of fabric to create feathers.

18 MAKING PUNCHED FEATHERS FOR WINGS + TAILS

Punched feathers, such as those shown on the lark on page 50, are fun to make. I began to punch fabric feathers using die-cut punch tools intended to be used by scrapbookers. These punch tools, which come in dozens of shapes, allow you to easily create rows of uniform feathers—several dozen leaf or hand shapes can be punched and layered together to look like feathers. If you're not able to find these paper-punch tools, cut individual feathers by hand; the imperfect shapes that free-form cutting creates can also be very beautiful. You'll also need fusible web (see page 12) to create punched feathers.

Begin by preparing fabric to be punched or cut into feathers. To make enough feathers for one bird, choose three pieces of fabric, about 10" x 16" (25.5 x 40.5 cm) each. Cut one of these fabrics into two 8" x 10" (20.5 x 25.5 cm) pieces and cut one

18a

piece of double-sided fusible web to the same size. Sandwich the fusible web between the two layers of fabric, with right sides of fabric facing out, and press to fuse the three layers, following the instructions for the fusible web. Repeat for the additional two fabrics.

Cut free-form feather shapes from the fused fabrics or, if you are using a punch, place the fused fabric on an old cutting mat. The mat may be damaged during punching, so if a mat isn't available, try a stack of newspapers. Place the punch on top and hit it several times with a hammer or rubber mallet. The punch will cut the fabric into the desired shape. You'll need several dozen feathers for each wing and tail. Whether free-form cutting or punching, try preparing several different colored or patterned fabrics and playing with how they look together.

Spray a sewn wing base with temporary fabric adhesive. Beginning at the bottom tip of the wing, position one feather in place, pressing down onto the sticky wing surface. Make two tiny handstitches at the top of the feather to hold it in place.

Now lay a second row of feathers above the first, overlapping them enough to hide the stitches securing the first feather. Sew the second row of feathers down with two tiny stitches at the top of each feather (fig. 18a).

Continue in this fashion until the entire wing is covered. Repeat with the other wing and the tail.

19a

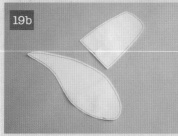

19b

19c

19d

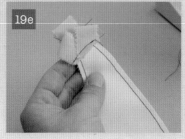

19e

19 MAKING FEATHERS FROM FABRIC LOOPS

The third basic method for creating feathers on wings and tails is to create loops with torn strips of fabric. I like to use quilting cotton to create loops because it tears very easily and in straight lines on either the lengthwise or the crosswise grain.

To tear strips, make a series of snips along one edge of a piece of fabric, about ½" (1.3 cm) apart (it is not important to be exact about this). Tear the fabric using the snips as starting points. Continue tearing until

you have a good pile of strips. Twelve to fifteen strips are needed for one wing, so several dozen in a few different colors will be needed to complete one bird (fig. 19a). You can press the strips if they are curled on the edges, but it is also fine to leave them as is. The curled edges will just add some volume to the finished feathers.

To begin sewing looped feathers, take a sewn wing base (fig. 19b) and make a single loop from the bottom of a torn strip. Hold or pin it in place at the bottom tip of the wing and then

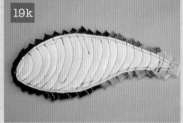

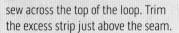

I prefer to form two or three loops at a time, sew across them, pause with the presser foot down to form a few more loops, sew across them, and continue.

Change loop colors periodically, perhaps after three or four rows of loops (**fig. 19h**).

Continue to form loops and stitch them down in rows partially overlapping the previous loops, until the entire wing is covered (**fig. 19i**). The stitched line that secures the top row of loops will show on the completed wing.

There will be a mass of threads hanging off the wing once all of the feathers have been sewn, including threads from stitching each row and threads from the torn fabric strips. I like these loose threads because they add to the feathery look of the wing (**fig. 19j**). I trim the long ones but keep many of the shorter ones. If you'd like a neater look, you can trim all of the threads.

The back of the wing will show the parallel lines of stitching used to attach the rows of feathers (**fig. 19k**). For a more subtle look, choose a thread color that matches the wing's base. I like the contrast of a bold thread color, because I think seeing evidence of the bird's construction adds interest to the finished piece.

Complete two wings, being sure the wings are mirror images of each other, and a tail for your bird.

sew across the top of the loop. Trim the excess strip just above the seam.

Using the same torn strip, form two loops and place them a bit higher up on the wing, but still overlapping the first loop enough to cover the stitching line (**fig. 19c**).

Stitch across the tops of these loops, securing them in place (**fig. 19d**). Trim just above the stitched line (**fig. 19e**).

As your strips run out, grab a new strip and form it into a loop and continue (**figs. 19f, 19g**). I find pins cumbersome to use during this process.

20a

20 ATTACH THE WINGS + TAIL TO THE BIRD BODY

Attaching the wings and tail to the bird body is always exciting, because you begin to see your vision as a fully formed bird for the first time. Attach the finished tail to the bird first, then one wing and then the other.

Pin the tail securely in place **(fig. 20a)**. Stand the bird up to check its balance; it may need some rebalancing because the center of gravity changes after the weight of the tail is added.

Using a strong needle and thread, tack the tail to the body or sew it using a neat ladder stitch, using invisible stitches spaced no more than about ½" (1.3 cm) apart.

I wear a thimble during this process because it can require some muscle, especially if the tail has been reinforced with interfacing.

Tie a good knot at the end to make sure the tail is firmly attached to the body.

Use the same process for attaching the wings, first pinning them in place to make sure you are happy with their position. They should be matched up so that they are even on both sides of the bird.

More rebalancing may be needed to make the bird successfully stand on its own after the wings are attached.

beaks

My preferred method for making beaks is to sew, turn, and stuff a fabric beak. This process is not everyone's cup of tea, however. It involves a good deal of practice and patience to maneuver the tiny pieces. There are easier and still very lovely methods for making a beak, such as using a small piece of felt or creating a polymer clay beak. The following sections describe my method for making a turned and stuffed fabric beak, an easy felt beak, and a polymer clay beak.

21 TURNED + STUFFED FABRIC BEAK

Although the fabric beak is my favorite, it's a little bit finicky to work with tiny pieces of fabric and tiny stitches. Be patient as you gain experience with this method.

Iron the beak pattern piece to a double layer of fabric, right sides together.

Leaving the bottom of the beak open for turning and stuffing, machine stitch around the pattern piece with very small stitches (about 16 stitches to 1" [2.5 cm]).

Remove the pattern piece and trim around the stitching line, leaving a scant ⅛" (3 mm) seam allowance. A narrow seam allowance is best for such a tiny pattern piece.

Insert forceps or craft tweezers to the tip of the beak and gently pull it right side out.

Fold the raw edges to the inside, press the turned-in edges flat, and baste **(fig. 21a)**. Basting is very helpful when sewing tiny things. Taking those few minutes to turn the raw edges inward and sewing them in place with a few basting stitches before stuffing means that later you will have an easier time achieving a neat edge when attaching that tiny piece to the larger sculpture.

Stuff the beak very firmly with tiny bits of stuffing **(fig. 21b)**.

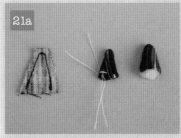

21a

21b

22a

You will notice on the beak pattern pieces that they never come to a sharp point. I learned a trick several years ago about creating sharply pointed features: don't create a sharply pointed pattern piece. Instead, flatten out the tip a bit, just enough to take one stitch across the point, as shown on the left in **fig. 21a**. When the beak is turned, there is less risk of tearing it when trying to force the point outward, and when it is stuffed it will actually appear more pointed than it would if the stitching had come to a sharp point.

22 FELT BEAK

Felt is a great material for simple beaks because it does not fray, so it

requires very little stitching. Simply fold over and iron a small square of wool felt and cut a triangle on the fold. Pin the beak to the bird and with one or two handstitches, or a bit of craft glue, attach it **(fig. 22a)**. Within a few minutes you have a simple, but still very appealing, bird beak.

23 CLAY BEAK

Polymer clay beaks can look very realistic and add interest to the finished bird by incorporating yet

23a

another texture and material. I used polymer clay with a little bit of sparkle for the beaks on each of my crows (page 56).

Pinch off a small piece of clay and roll it into a little cone. Curve the bottom a bit so that it will rest flush with the fabric of the bird's face and then bake the clay according to the package directions **(fig. 23a)**.

Lightly sand the clay if fingerprints are still visible after baking.

To change the color of the beak or add some painted detail, paint the beak after baking with acrylic paint. For a shiny finish, glaze with an acrylic sealer such as Mod Podge.

Hold the beak up to the bird to figure out exact placement. Use a dab of E6000 or another very strong craft glue to affix the beak to the fabric.

eyes

I think that the appeal of all soft toys and fabric sculpture really comes down to the eyes. This is where the viewer first looks and decides whether the finished piece is appealing or not. Eyes can be very tiny or big and round, spread apart or close together, with lashes or brows or without, low on the face or way up top. They can be formed with embroidery stitches, felt, beads, paint, washers, or scraps of fabric.

The placement, size, and material used for the eyes require a good deal of thought, and I often find myself pulling out the first attempt because I am not satisfied. The heads of pins are very useful when planning eyes. Place pins where you think the eye might go and then walk away from the bird. Look at the bird from several feet away. Are the eyes evoking the expression you are hoping for? If not, move the pins.

The eyes can also appear differently once the beak is in place. I like to place the beak level with the eyes;

to me, this makes the bird look sweet and appealing. I also like the eyes spaced fairly far apart. Experiment! Try an owl with closed eyes or a quail with long lashes. Whatever your choice, remember that the eyes are the first area of focus for the viewer, and they need to be well executed. The following sections describe my method for embroidered eyes and bead eyes.

24 EMBROIDERED EYES

Embroidery is my favorite technique for making eyes **(fig. 24a)**. It gives you flexibility in terms of the size and shape of the eye, without the permanence of painting the eye on or drawing it with fabric markers. For the projects in this book, I use several neutral shades of six-strand cotton embroidery floss for eyes, including off-white, light and dark brown, and black.

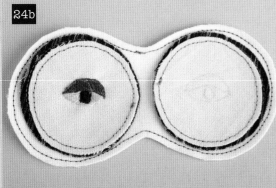

To embroider an eye, begin by sketching the eye on the fabric with a disappearing ink fabric marker **(fig. 24b)**. The photographs show an owl's eye mask.

Cut an 18" (45.5 cm) length of floss and pull out two of the six strands. Thread an embroidery needle with both strands and tie a small tight knot at the end.

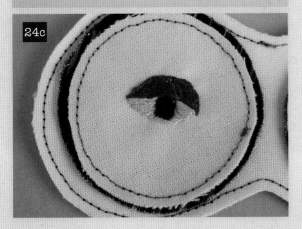

If you're sewing directly onto a bird's body, insert the needle some distance away, where the beak will be, and give the end a gentle tug to pull the knot inside.

25a

25b

If you're embroidering on a circle base that will be layered onto another circle, such as for owls, the knot can remain on the back of the circle base.

Begin by outlining the eyeball using a backstitch.

Fill it in with satin stitch and draw brows or lashes with stem stitch (fig. 24c).

25 USE BEADS FOR EYES

Sewing on beads for eyes is a fast and simple method that still makes an appealing look. I prefer to use round black beads that are a bit larger than seed beads (fig. 25a). The following method works best if the eyes are stitched before the beak is attached.

Place pins where you would like the eyes to be.

Thread a needle with a double length of black thread and insert it where the beak will be. Give it a tug to pull the knot inside the bird and bring the needle out where you have placed a pin.

Pass the needle through the hole in the bead and then directly under the bead through a few threads of the fabric. Go through the fabric and the bead a few more times to secure the bead, then tie a knot that will be hidden underneath the bead.

Repeat for the other eye.

Pass the needle out of the bird at the beak and trim the end of the thread, pulling it into the bird to hide the thread tails.

Bead eyes can also be sewn to an eye mask before the mask is tacked to the bird's head (fig. 25b).

designing your own patterns

Once you've sewn up a few fabric birds from patterns in this book, you may want to try designing an original bird pattern. Perhaps you'd like to make a blue jay, a robin, a parrot, or another bird that strikes your fancy. It may take a few tries, but designing an original pattern is very satisfying, and the finished bird will be truly your own. Follow these steps:

1 Begin by looking at images of birds, either in nature guides, online, or from your own photographs. It's important to refer to a profile photo of the bird you'd like to make.

2 Cut a piece of freezer paper somewhat larger than you'd like the side body pattern piece to be.

3 Make a light pencil drawing of the bird's profile to get the basic shapes, then go back and darken the pencil lines when you are more certain of the accuracy of the drawing. This will be the side body pattern piece. Be sure to label all of your pattern pieces as you go.

4 Draw a line from the tip of the tail, across the side body, to the breast. The line can dip downward a bit when it is above the legs and curve upward a bit as nears the breast. Everything below the line will be the underbody pattern piece. You will need to lay a second piece of freezer paper on top of your drawing now to retrace the underbody so that it will be its own pattern piece.

5 If the bird is going to be large, draw a horizontal football-shaped dart at the top of each leg so that the legs will not splay outward when stuffed.

surface design techniques for wings

Embellishing the wings of a bird is one of the most exciting parts of fabric birdmaking. The basic instructions offered here include methods for quilted wings and for wings with looped or punched fabric feathers, but the wings and tails of birds are perfect for experimenting with many more surface design techniques, such as those shown below.

Column 1, from top: lace overlay; smocked fabric; looped sheer ribbon. **Column 2,** from top: lace overlay; cut-up book pages; glued seed beads. **Column 3,** from top: free-motion embroidery; glued rhinestones; acrylic paint; fabric yo-yos.

6 Measure along the top of the head with a measuring tape to determine how long the head gusset should be. Draw a pointed oval that length for the head gusset. Make sure the oval is relatively narrow or the head will be distorted.

7 Sketch the wings, tail, and beak on the freezer paper. Label all of your pattern pieces and include any markings where you need to leave openings for turning and stuffing.

8 Cut out all your pattern pieces.

9 Sew up the first draft of your new bird with inexpensive muslin and stuff it with polyester fiberfill (instead of the more expensive wool) because there are bound to be parts of the pattern that will need some adjustment. Once your first draft is sewn, stuffed, and standing, walk away from it and come back later with fresh eyes. Notice areas that look out of proportion and redraw some or all of the pattern pieces to make adjustments.

10 Sew up a second draft in muslin or in nicer fabrics if you are confident that the bird will now be to your liking.

projects

NOW THAT YOU'VE EXPLORED my basic birdmaking techniques, you can use them to make any of the sixteen projects that follow, from a sweet little wren to a ponderous owl, a graceful flying gull, an elegant flamingo, and many more. Choose fabrics and colors that you love and try different ways to embellish wings and tails and embroider eyes to give your birds unique personalities. I hope you'll love making these birds and get many hours of pleasure from these projects. Beginning on page 128, you'll also find interviews and photographs of work from four of today's leading fabric-bird artists to inspire you even more and to help you see the limitless possibilities of fabric birdmaking.

As you choose your first bird project, be sure to refer back to Basic Birdmaking Techniques, pages 19 to 39, for detailed explanations of each step of the process. You'll find pattern templates for all of the projects beginning on page 138. Where necessary, you'll find illustrations with the project instructions for steps that are unique to a particular project. If you're not sure where to start, the Wren, page 46, is a good basic pattern that will give you a feel for the process that you can then apply to more complex birds. Most important, have fun, take your time, enjoy the pleasure of working with fabric, thread, and wire, and give your creative imagination free rein; you can't go wrong!

bird in a nest

I never pass up the chance to buy wooden spools of thread at rummage sales, though the thread is too brittle for sewing. I display empty spools in my studio with birds perched on them and keep full spools in a basket where I can admire the colors and labels. The threads in the basket tend to get tangled, and one day I was inspired to make more of a tangle, pulling threads from many spools at once and winding them around a wire frame to create a bird's nest of vintage thread. A bit of wool roving creates a nice soft lining and a sleepy baby bird rests inside.

FINISHED SIZE
Nest, 3¼" (8.5 cm) in diameter and 1¼" (3.2 cm) tall; bird, 4¾" (12 cm) from beak to tail

MATERIALS
Cotton fabric for bird body, ¼ yd (23 cm)

3 different cotton fabrics for feathers, ¼ yd (23 cm) total

Scrap of brown felt for beak

Wool stuffing, 4 oz (114 g)

Brown embroidery floss

Spools of thread in various colors for nest (I used vintage thread unsuited for sewing)

Small handful of wool roving in coordinating color

18-gauge aluminum wire, 18" (45.5 cm), for nest armature

TOOLS
Basic birdmaking tool kit

PATTERN PIECES (page 138)
Side Body (cut 1, cut 1 reverse)

Head Gusset (cut 1)

Wing (cut 2, cut 2 reverse)

Tail (cut 2)

NOTES
● Before you begin, read Basic Birdmaking Techniques, pages 19–39, for detailed instructions on the birdmaking process.

● Add ¼" (6 mm) seam allowance to all pattern pieces except where noted.

1 Prewash and iron all fabrics. Trace pattern pieces onto freezer paper. Be sure to cut left and right versions of Side Body and Wing pattern pieces.

2 Iron freezer paper patterns to fabric, matte side up, and cut left and right Side Body pieces and one Head Gusset from bird body fabric. Transfer all markings.

3 Pin Head Gusset to top of head on one Side Body, right sides together. Sew from point A to point B. Pin other side of Head Gusset to other Side Body and sew from point A to point B.

4 Sew the rest of the body together, leaving a 1" (2.5 cm) opening for turning and stuffing, as indicated on pattern.

5 Clip all curves. Use forceps to gently pull the tail and then the head into the body. Gently turn the bird right side out through the opening, pulling the head through the opening first. Use forceps to push the tail out. Stuff the bird with small pieces of stuffing, beginning at the head and working your way down, packing the stuffing very firmly as you go. Close the opening with ladder stitch.

6 Using Wing and Tail pattern pieces, make bases for two wings and one tail and embellish with fabric-loop feathers.

7 Pin tail to bird. Tack down with a few handstitches at the top of the tail, using ladder stitch or your preferred handstitch. Pin wings to bird. Tack down along the top of the wing.

8 Fold the scrap of brown felt in half and press. On the fold, cut a small triangle. Put

bird tail

bird beak + eyes

a small dab of craft glue on the outside folded edge of the beak and press it onto the bird's face. Pin in place until the glue dries.

9 Draw the eyes with disappearing ink fabric marker. Stitch with two strands of brown embroidery floss using stem stitch (see page 137).

completed nest

11 Gather about five spools of vintage thread. Hold all five of the thread ends in one hand and begin pulling the thread off the spools. Gather the thread in a tangle as you pull. Once you have a good handful of thread, begin to wrap it around the interior of the spiral to form the base of the nest. Continue to pull thread off the spools and wrap it around the wire armature, working your way up and out. Be sure to cover the wire that will be inside the nest as well as the wire that will be on the outside. Once the nest is mostly covered, cut the thread ends. Thread a needle and stitch intermittently around the nest to secure the thread tangle and ensure that the entire wire armature is covered.

10 To create the nest, form a loose spiral with an 18" (45.5 cm) length of 18-gauge aluminum wire **(fig. 1)**. Pull the spiral upward so that the center rests on the work surface and the wide outside ring is a few inches above the work surface. The wire will serve as the armature for the nest **(fig. 2)**.

12 Gather a small handful of wool roving. Rub it in your palms to form it into a loose circular wad. Place roving inside nest to create a fluffy down. Rest bird in nest.

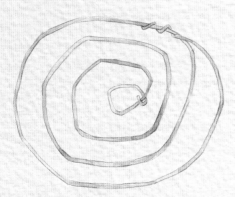

fig. 1: form a loose spiral with 18-gauge wire for the nest.

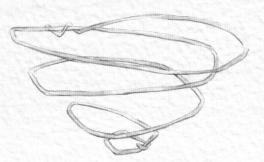

fig.2: pull the spiral upward to create the nest armature.

Wren

This is a good basic bird pattern; if you master it, the other birds in this book will come relatively easily. The wings are quilted, offering an opportunity to do some creative stitching, and the finished wren is just about life-size. If you choose a realistic color palette, this wren could even be mistaken for a live bird. The small size of the wren makes it well suited to a series or even an installation. Try bending a wren's toes around a tree branch or setting up a group of wrens on tiers of vintage wooden spools.

FINISHED SIZE
4½" (11.5 cm) tall

MATERIALS
Brown or gold fabric for lower part of body, ⅛ yd (11.5 cm)

Lighter fabric for upper part of body, ⅛ yd (11.5 cm)

Scrap of fabric or small scrap of felt for beak

Scraps of fabric for wings to total ⅛ yd (11.5 cm)

Wool stuffing, 8 oz (227 g)

Cotton batting, ⅛ yd (11.5 cm)

16-gauge brass wire, 36" (91.5 cm)

Black or brown floral tape

Dark brown embroidery floss

TOOLS
Basic birdmaking tool kit

PATTERN PIECES (page 139)
Side Body (cut 1, cut 1 reverse, from pieced fabric)

Underbody (cut 1, cut 1 reverse)

Head Gusset (cut 1)

Tail (cut 2)

Beak (cut as directed)

Lower Wing (cut as directed)

Middle Wing (cut as directed)

Upper Wing (cut as directed)

NOTES
- Before you begin, read Basic Birdmaking Techniques, pages 19–39, for detailed instructions on the birdmaking process.
- Add ¼" (6 mm) seam allowance to all pattern pieces except where noted.

1 Prewash and iron all fabrics. Trace pattern pieces onto freezer paper. Be sure to cut left and right versions of Side Body, Underbody, Lower Wing, Middle Wing, and Upper Wing pattern pieces.

2 With right sides together, stitch the brown fabric to the lighter fabric along the long edge. Press seam toward the brown fabric. Trim seam allowance to about ⅛" (3 mm).

3 Press Side Body pattern piece, matte side up, to wrong side of single layer of pieced fabric, aligning line on pattern piece with seam on fabric so that brown fabric is bird's body and lighter fabric is bird's face and head. Cut out, then flip fabric over and repeat.

4 Press freezer paper patterns to fabric, matte side up, and cut left and right Underbody pieces and Head Gusset from brown fabric. Transfer all markings.

5 Pin Underbody pieces, right sides together, along top edge. Stitch from point A to point B and from point C to point D, leaving a 1" (2.5 cm) opening in the center of the seam for turning and stuffing.

6 Pin one Underbody to one Side Body, right sides together. Stitch along the bottom of the bird, leaving an opening at the base of the leg for inserting wire. Repeat with other Underbody and Side Body so that the bottom of the wren is now sewn.

7 Pin Head Gusset to one Side Body, right sides together. Sew from point E to point F. Pin other side of Head Gusset to other Side Body and sew from point E to point F.

8 Sew remaining body seams (from point A to point F and then from point E to point D) so that now the wren's body is sewn completely, with an opening for turning and stuffing on the underbody seam and openings at the bottom of each leg for inserting the wire.

9 Clip all curves, especially near the legs. Reinforce seams with additional stitching if needed. Use forceps to gently pull the legs into the body, then the tail, and finally the head. Gently turn the wren right side out through the opening left in the underbody seam, pulling the head through the opening first. Use forceps to push the legs and tail out. Stuff the wren with small pieces of stuffing, beginning at the head and working your way down, packing the stuffing very firmly as you go.

10 When you have about ½" (1.3 mm) remaining to stuff at the bottom of the wren, pause and insert the 16-gauge wire for the legs and feet.

11 Finish stuffing, pushing small bits of stuffing into the body to cover the wire and hold it in place. Push stuffing bit by bit into the leg openings and the tail. Push as much stuffing into the wren as possible.

12 Form the feet. Each leg should be about 1" (2.5 cm) long, and each toe should be about ½" (1.3 cm) long. Balance the bird.

13 Push a bit more stuffing into body to hold legs in place and close the opening with ladder stitch. Wrap the legs and feet with floral tape.

14 To make the quilted wings, cut a piece of cotton batting about the same size as the Lower Wing pattern piece. Place two scraps of brown

wren three-part quilted wings

wren beak + eye, front view

wren tail + wings, rear view

fabric, right sides together, on top of batting. Iron the Lower Wing pattern piece on top of all layers and stitch around pattern piece, leaving an opening for turning. Pull off the pattern piece and trim ⅛" (3 mm) from stitching line. Turn wing right side out so that batting is sandwiched inside. Fold raw edges of opening inward and press. Handstitch the opening closed with ladder stitch. Repeat for other Lower Wing. Repeat this process with the Middle Wings, Upper Wings, and Tail.

15 Draw feathery lines on each wing and tail with disappearing fabric marker. Quilt the design you've made by hand or machine to evoke feathers.

16 Pin finished tail to bird and tack down with a few handstitches, using ladder stitch or your preferred handstitch. Pin lower wings to bird and tack down, then overlap middle wings and upper wings slightly and tack down each wing with a few handstitches.

17 Iron Beak pattern piece to the wrong side of a double layer of fabric. Sew around pattern

piece, leaving base of beak open for turning and stuffing.

18 Trim close to stitching and pull pattern piece off. Turn beak right side out gently using forceps. Turn raw edges of beak inward and baste. Stuff beak firmly. Pin and sew beak to wren with ladder stitch or your preferred handstitch. Alternatively, make a small felt beak as described on page 36.

19 Draw eyes with disappearing ink fabric marker. Using two strands of embroidery floss, embroider eyeball with satin stitch and eyebrows, if desired, with stem stitch (see page 137).

lark

A few years ago, I made a rag doll with a head that was constructed like a baseball, with a front panel and two curved side panels, only to find that the head was too small for the doll. Weeks later, I was working on creating a bird whose head could look in any direction. I grabbed the discarded doll head and sewed a bird body to match. The result is a wonderfully flexible design that allows you to create a little bird that can look up at a falling leaf, search the ground for seeds, or glance shyly at another bird by its side.

FINISHED SIZE
6½" (16.5 cm) tall

MATERIALS
White or neutral fabric for bird body, ¼ yd (23 cm)

3 colorful fabrics for feathers and eye mask, ¼ yd (23 cm) each

Scrap of brown fabric for beak

Wool stuffing, 10 oz (283.5 g)

16-gauge brass wire, 36" (91.5 cm)

Dark brown floral tape

2 small round black beads

Double-sided fusible web, three 8" × 10" (20.5 × 25.5 cm) sheets

TOOLS
Basic birdmaking tool kit

Optional: Leaf-shaped craft punch, old cutting mat or stack of newspapers, and hammer

PATTERN PIECES (page 140)
Side Body (cut 1, cut 1 reverse)

Underbody (cut 1, cut 1 reverse)

Side Head (cut 2)

Head Gusset (cut 1)

Tail (cut 2)

Wing (cut 2, cut 2 reverse)

Eye Mask (cut as directed)

Eye Overlay (cut as directed)

Beak (cut as directed)

NOTES
◆ Before you begin, read Basic Birdmaking Techniques, pages 19–39, for detailed instructions on the birdmaking process.

◆ Add ¼" (6 mm) seam allowance to all pattern pieces except where noted.

lark
legs + feet

1 Prewash and iron all fabrics. Trace pattern pieces onto freezer paper and cut out. Be sure to cut left and right versions of Side Body, Underbody, and Wing pattern pieces.

2 Iron freezer paper patterns to fabric, matte side up, and cut left and right Side Body pieces, left and right Underbody pieces, one Head Gusset, and two Side Head pieces from bird body fabric. Transfer all markings.

3 Sew an oval dart as indicated on each Under-body piece. Fold legs down and pin to keep them out of the way.

4 Pin Underbody pieces, right sides together, along top edge. Stitch from point A to point B and from point C to point D, leaving a 1" (2.5 cm) opening in the center of the seam for turning and stuffing.

5 Pin one Underbody to one Side Body, right sides together, with the dart pointed upward. Stitch bottom of bird, leaving the base of the leg open for inserting wire. Repeat with other Underbody and Side Body so that the bottom of the lark is now sewn. Sew the rest of the way around the body; you will have an opening between the underbodies for turning and stuffing, and at the base of each leg for inserting the wire.

6 Clip all curves, especially near the legs. Reinforce seams with additional stitching as needed. Use forceps to gently pull the legs into the body, then the tail, and finally the neck. Gently turn the lark right side out through the opening left in the underbody seam, pulling the neck through the opening first. Use forceps to push the legs and tail out. Stuff the lark's body with small pieces of stuffing, beginning at the neck and working your way down, packing the stuffing very firmly as you go. When you have about ½" (1.3 mm) of the bird remaining to be stuffed, pause to insert the 16-gauge wire.

7 Finish stuffing, pushing small bits of stuffing into the body to cover the wire and hold it in place. Push stuffing bit by bit into the leg openings and the tail. Push as much stuffing into the lark as possible.

8 Make the feet. The total length of the finished leg should be about 1½" (3.8 cm). The total length of the longest toe should be about 1" (2.5 cm). Balance the bird so it stands on its own.

9 Push a bit more stuffing into the bird's body and close the opening with ladder stitch. Wrap the legs and feet with floral tape.

10 Pin Head Gusset to one Side Head piece. Sew from point E to point F. Repeat with other Side Head piece so that the head is now sewn.

11 Clip curves on head and turn right side out using forceps to reach inside the head and gently grasp the fabric, pulling it through the opening. Stuff the head firmly through the opening where the "neck" will be inserted. Turn raw edges inward and baste.

12 Push the head onto the neck and pin in place with regular pins. Head can be tilted or turned in any direction. Sew head to neck with tiny neat ladder stitches or your preferred handstitch **(fig. 1)**. Balance the bird.

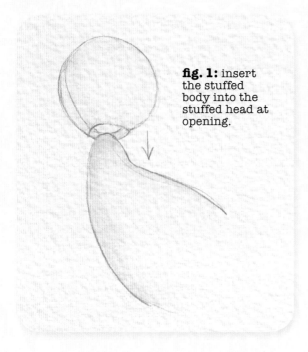

fig. 1: insert the stuffed body into the stuffed head at opening.

13 Cut a double layer of decorative fabric ¼" (6 mm) larger than each Eye Mask piece. Place wrong sides together (these are not turned) and iron Eye Mask pattern pieces to doubled fabric. Machine stitch directly around the freezer paper. Pull off the freezer paper and trim ⅛" (3 mm) from stitching line.

14 Cut a double layer of body fabric ¼" (6 mm) larger than each Eye Overlay. With wrong sides of fabric together (these are not turned), iron Eye Overlay pattern pieces on top of the doubled fabric. Machine stitch around the freezer paper. Pull off the freezer paper and trim ⅛" (3 mm) from stitching line.

15 Place one Eye Overlay onto one Eye Mask. Pin. Tack Eye Overlay to Eye Mask. Sew bead in the center of the Eye Overlay. Repeat for other Eye Mask.

16 Place completed eyes onto the lark's head and pin in place. Tack down with a few small ladder stitches or your preferred handstitch.

17 Press Beak pattern piece onto a double layer of fabric, right sides together. Machine stitch around pattern piece with very small stitches, leaving bottom of beak open. Trim close to stitching. Pull off pattern piece. Turn beak right side out, turn raw edge under and baste, and stuff. Pin and sew beak in place with ladder stitch or your preferred handstitch.

18 Use the Wing and Tail pattern pieces to create bases for the wings and tail.

lark

lark eyes + beak

lark punched feathers, rear view

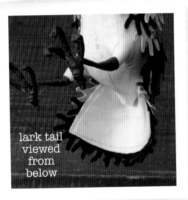

lark tail viewed from below

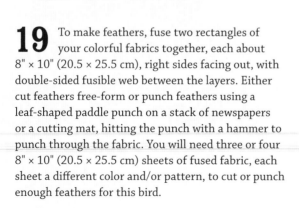

19 To make feathers, fuse two rectangles of your colorful fabrics together, each about 8" × 10" (20.5 × 25.5 cm), right sides facing out, with double-sided fusible web between the layers. Either cut feathers free-form or punch feathers using a leaf-shaped paddle punch on a stack of newspapers or a cutting mat, hitting the punch with a hammer to punch through the fabric. You will need three or four 8" × 10" (20.5 × 25.5 cm) sheets of fused fabric, each sheet a different color and/or pattern, to cut or punch enough feathers for this bird.

20 Spray one side of both wing bases and tail base with a light coating of spray adhesive. Beginning at the tip of the tail and the tips of the wings, place a feather and stitch it down with one or two handstitches at the top of the feather. For the second row, place two feathers overlapping the top of the first row and handstitch each one down. Continue this way, covering both wings and the tail with feathers.

21 Pin tail to stuffed lark body and tack down with a few ladder stitches or your preferred handstitch. Pin wings to lark body and tack down in the same manner.

MAKING A BIRD FROM HAND-DYED FABRICS

One way to make a totally unique bird is to use fabrics you dye yourself. Don't be intimidated by fabric dyes. They're easy to use, and the results are always interesting. Add this technique to your creative repertoire. For a simple first experience with creating hand-dyed fabrics for a bird project, make gradients of a single color. You can then make quilted wings or use torn strips from each gradient to create feathers on a bird's wings and tail.

I use a readily available fabric dye such as Rit or Dylon. You only need one pouch of dye for this project, so choose a color you love.

1 Select 1 yard (91.5 cm) of white tightly woven quilting cotton fabric. Prewash the fabric and then cut or tear it into four equal pieces.

2 Create a dyebath in a large bucket, pot, or your kitchen sink following the package instructions. Set one of the four fabric pieces aside. This one will stay white. Put the other three pieces into the dyebath, give them a quick swirl to make sure the fabric is saturated, and then immediately pull one piece out.

Rinse this piece in cold water until the water runs clear.

3 After about a minute, pull a second piece out of the dyebath and rinse thoroughly in cold water.

4 Wait about 15 minutes, and then pull out the final piece of fabric. Rinse it thoroughly in cold water.

5 Machine dry the three dyed fabrics and press, then get started making a bird! Use the white fabric for the head so that the eyes show up well and use the dyed fabrics for stunning wings.

6 When you're ready to get more adventurous, sew a bird body and turn it right side out. Dip the body into a dyebath and pull it out a little at a time so that various gradations of color are left on the fabric. Rinse, dry, and stuff the bird.

Crow

Crows are mysterious but highly intelligent birds; their dark feathers and screeching calls give them an air of danger. A group of crows is called a murder; huddled together, all in black, a murder of fabric crows adds a gothic accent to a room. I like the energy of a grouping of crows in action, with some taking flight and some alighting, as though they are enacting a secret plot together. Try to capture a knowing yet mysterious facial expression. Silver embroidery floss gives the eyes a bit of sparkle, and a polymer clay beak adds some textural variation to the finished bird.

FINISHED SIZE
Sizes vary; flying crow has a 12" (30.5 cm) wingspan and is 9" (23 cm) from front of head to tip of tail. Crow taking off is 9" (23 cm) tall.

MATERIALS
Dark fabric for body, wings, and tail, ½ yd (45.5 cm)

Wool stuffing, 10 oz (284 g)

16-gauge brass wire, 36" (91.5 cm)

Black floral tape (or any floral tape and black acrylic paint)

Silver embroidery floss

Black polymer clay, one 2-ounce (57 g) package

TOOLS
Basic birdmaking tool kit

Small paintbrush

Lightweight sandpaper

White tailor's chalk

PATTERN PIECES (page 141)
Side Body (cut 1, cut 1 reverse)

Underbody (cut 1, cut 1 reverse)

Head Gusset (cut 1)

Tail (cut 2)

Wing (see Notes; cut 2, cut 2 reverse)

NOTES
● Before you begin, read Basic Birdmaking Techniques, pages 19–39, for detailed instructions on the birdmaking process.

● Add ¼" (6 mm) seam allowance to all pattern pieces except where noted.

● Use the Crow Wing pattern piece for standing crows.

● Use the Gull Wing pattern piece on page 154 for flying crows and follow Gull instructions for shaping flying wings (page 114).

● Use the Crow Tail pattern for either standing or flying crows.

crow legs
+ feet

1 Prewash and iron all fabrics. Trace pattern pieces onto freezer paper and cut out. Be sure to cut left and right versions of Side Body, Underbody, and Wing.

2 Iron freezer paper patterns to fabric, matte side up, and cut left and right Side Body pieces, left and right Underbody pieces, and one Head Gusset from bird body fabric. Transfer all markings.

3 Sew oval darts on each Underbody piece. Fold legs down and pin down to keep them out of the way.

4 Pin Underbody pieces, right sides together, along top edge. Stitch from point A to point B and from point C to point D, leaving a 1" (2.5 cm) opening in the center of the seam for turning and stuffing.

5 Pin one Underbody to one Side Body, right sides together, with the dart pointed upward. Stitch along the bottom of the bird, leaving an opening at the base of the leg for inserting wire. Repeat with other Underbody and Side Body so that the bottom of the crow is now sewn.

6 Pin Head Gusset to top of head on one Side Body, right sides together. Sew from point E to point F. Pin other side of Head Gusset to other Side Body and sew from point E to point F.

7 Sew remaining body seams (from point A to point F and then from point E to point D) so that now the crow's body is sewn completely, with an opening for turning and stuffing on the underbody seam and openings at the base of each leg for inserting the wire.

8 Clip all curves, especially near the legs. Reinforce seams with additional stitching as needed. Use forceps to gently pull the legs into the body, then the tail of the bird, and finally the head. Gently turn the crow right side out through the opening left in the underbody seam, pulling the head through the opening first. Use forceps to push the legs and tail out. Stuff the crow with small pieces of stuffing, beginning at the head and working your way down, packing the stuffing very firmly as you go.

9 When you've stuffed about three-fourths of the bird body, pause to insert the wire for the legs and feet. After placing the wire, finish stuffing, pushing small bits of stuffing into the body to cover the wire and hold it in place. Push stuffing bit by bit into the leg openings and the tail. Push as much stuffing into the crow as possible.

10 Form the feet. The total length of each finished leg should be about 1¾" (4.5 cm). The total length of the longest toe should be about 1" (2.5 cm). Balance the bird.

11 Push a bit more stuffing into the bird's body and close the opening with ladder stitch. Wrap the legs and feet with floral tape. If floral tape is not black, paint it black with acrylic paint and let dry completely. Seal with an acrylic sealer such as Mod Podge.

12 Using Wing and Tail pattern pieces, make bases for wings and tail. Sew rows of looped feathers to cover wings and tail. Pin tail to crow and tack down. Pin wings to crow and tack down. Balance the bird again.

13 Condition the polymer clay by kneading it until soft. Pull off a small piece and form it into a triangle. Curve the tip of the triangle downward slightly. Gently push the base of the beak against the crow's face to shape it, indenting the base of the beak slightly so that it will lay flush against the crow's face. Bake the clay according to the package instructions. Let cool. Lightly sand to erase any fingerprints. With a paintbrush, coat beak with acrylic sealer. Coat base of beak with a thin layer of E6000 adhesive and press beak to crow's head. Hold in place until thoroughly dry.

14 Mark placement of eyes with tailor's chalk. Using two strands of silver embroidery floss, embroider eyes with long straight stitches to create a fan shape.

underside of crow wings

crow beak + eyes

quail

Quails are small, plump birds that nest on the ground. Whimsical head feathers and colorful plumage make this an especially attractive finished piece. I like to give the quail long flirty eyelashes to add to its allure. Because this bird is a ground dweller, it doesn't stand on wire legs; its rotund body is weighted with a smooth stone inserted during stuffing so that it stays upright.

FINISHED SIZE

5½" (14 cm) tall

MATERIALS

White cotton fabric for body, ¼ yd (23 cm)

Scraps of colorful cotton for wings, crest, and tail, to total ¼ yd (23 cm) of fabric

Scrap of brown cotton fabric for beak, 3" × 3" (7.5 × 7.5 cm)

Wool stuffing, 10 oz (283.5 g)

Brown embroidery floss

18-gauge aluminum wire for crest, 15" (38 cm)

Smooth stone for weight, about 1½" (3.8 cm) in diameter

TOOLS

Basic birdmaking tool kit

Optional: Round craft punch, cutting mat or stack of newspapers, and hammer

PATTERN PIECES (page 142)

Side Body (cut 1, cut 1 reverse)

Bottom Gusset (cut 1)

Head Gusset (cut 1)

Wing (cut 2, cut 2 reverse)

Tail (cut 2)

Beak (cut as directed)

NOTES

● Before you begin, read Basic Birdmaking Techniques, pages 19–39, for detailed instructions on the birdmaking process.

● Add ¼" (6 mm) seam allowance to all pattern pieces except where noted.

quail

quail wings +bottom gusset construction, front view

quail tail with multicolored looped feathers

1 Prewash and iron all fabrics. Trace pattern pieces onto freezer paper and cut out.

2 Iron a Side Body pattern piece onto a double layer of white cotton fabric. Adding ¼" (6 mm) seam allowance, cut out through both layers. Transfer all markings. Trace Bottom Gusset and Head Gusset onto freezer paper and iron onto a single layer of white cotton fabric. Cut, adding ¼" (6 mm) seam allowance. Transfer all markings.

3 Pin Bottom Gusset to one Side Body from point A to point B. Stitch. Pin remaining edge of Bottom Gusset to other Side Body from point A to point B. Stitch.

4 Pin Head Gusset to one Side Body from point C to point D and stitch. Pin remaining edge of Head Gusset to other Side Body from point C to point D and sew.

5 Sew remainder of bird between point A and point C and between point B and point D, leaving the marked opening for turning and stuffing unsewn.

6 Clip curves and reinforce seams as needed. Turn quail right side out with forceps, pulling head into body first and then pulling the rest of the body through the opening.

7 Stuff quail with small pieces of stuffing, beginning at the head and working your way down, packing the stuffing very firmly as you go.

8 About ¼" (6 mm) from the bottom of the quail, pause to insert your smooth stone. Push stone into body, keeping it parallel with the bottom of the bird. Surround the stone with stuffing and finish stuffing the quail. Push as much stuffing into the quail as possible, checking to make sure the bird balances upright and readjusting the position of the stone as needed to maintain balance.

9 Close the opening with ladder stitch or your preferred handstitch.

10 Using Wing and Tail pattern pieces, make bases for two wings and one tail from white cotton fabric. Note that this Tail has a dart for shaping; after ironing the pattern piece to a double layer of fabric, stitch around the pattern piece. Trace the dart with fabric marker. Pull the pattern piece off. Sew the dart. Snip off the excess fabric from the dart.

quail profile, showing crest + eye

11 Create looped wings and tail with strips of colorful torn cotton fabric. Pin tail to quail and tack in place. Pin wings to quail and tack in place with ladder stitch or your preferred handstitch.

12 Iron Beak pattern piece to the wrong side of a double layer of brown fabric. Sew around pattern piece, leaving base of beak open. Trim close to stitching and pull pattern piece off. Turn beak right side out, turn raw edges of beak under, baste, and stuff. Pin beak to quail's face and handstitch with ladder stitch or your preferred handstitch.

13 Draw eye and eyelashes with disappearing fabric marker. Using two strands of brown embroidery floss, embroider the eyes with satin stitch (see page 137) and lashes with straight stitch.

14 To make the crest, cut three lengths of 18-gauge aluminum wire, each 2½" (6.5 cm) long. Fold each length of wire in half. Poke wire through quail's head so that fold in wire is buried inside head and ends of wire stick out. There will be six wire ends sticking out of quail's head all together. Use a dab of craft glue at the base of each wire where it emerges from the quail's head to hold it in place. Let glue dry completely.

15 Cut twelve small circles from colorful cotton fabric, or use the circular craft punch, punching circles on a stack of old newspapers or a cutting mat, and hitting the punch with a hammer to punch through the fabric. Apply a dab of glue to two circles. Sandwich the end of the first length of wire between the two circles and press to adhere. Repeat for all six lengths of wire to create the crest.

Chick

To design this project, I sorted through my bins of fabric, searching for something that suggested the downy fluff of a new-born chick. I settled on a soft piece of yellow terry cloth for the chick's body and white faux fur for the wings. Terry cloth was a new bird fabric for me, but it works surprisingly well. Choose a lightweight terry with no stretch and you will find it sews up just as well as quilting cotton. The simple folded felt beak and bead eye make the chick look as though it is chirping.

FINISHED SIZE
4¼" (11 cm) tall

MATERIALS
Lightweight terry cloth for body, ¼ yd (23 cm)

Scrap of white fur fabric for top of wings, about 6" × 6" (15 × 15 cm)

Scrap of white cotton fabric for underside of wings, about 6" × 6" (15 × 15 cm)

Scrap of brown wool felt for beak

Wool stuffing, 7 oz (198 g)

16-gauge brass wire, 36" (91.5 cm)

White floral tape

Yellow and white acrylic paints

2 round black beads for eyes

Black thread

TOOLS
Basic birdmaking tool kit

Beading needle

PATTERN PIECES (page 158)
Side Body (cut 1, cut 1 reverse)

Underbody (cut 1, cut 1 reverse)

Back Gusset (cut 1)

Head (cut 1, cut 1 reverse)

Head Gusset (cut 1)

Wing (from cotton, cut 1, cut 1 reverse; from fur, cut 1, cut 1 reverse)

Beak (cut as directed)

NOTES
● Before you begin, read Basic Birdmaking Techniques, pages 19–39, for detailed instructions on the birdmaking process.

● Add ¼" (6 mm) seam allowance to all pattern pieces except where noted.

1 Prewash and iron all fabrics. Trace pattern pieces onto freezer paper. Be sure to cut left and right versions of Side Body, Underbody, Head, and Wings.

2 Iron freezer paper pattern pieces onto fabric and cut two Side Body pieces, two Underbody pieces, two Head pieces, a Head Gusset, and a Back Gusset from terry cloth. Cut a left and right Wing from fur and a left and right Wing from cotton. Transfer all markings.

3 Pin Underbody pieces, right sides together, along top edge. Stitch along top edge from point A to point B and from point C to point D, leaving a 1" (2.5 cm) opening in the center of the seam for turning and stuffing.

4 Pin one Underbody to one Side Body, right sides together. Stitch along bottom of bird, leaving an opening at the base of the leg for inserting the wire. Repeat with other Underbody and Side Body.

5 Pin Head Gusset to Head, right sides together, and stitch from point F to point G. Pin other side of Head Gusset to other Head piece and sew from point F to point G. Finish sewing head, leaving bottom open for turning. Turn head right side out.

6 Pin Back Gusset to one Side Body, right sides together, from point D to point E. Sew from point D to point E. Pin other side of Back Gusset to Side Body and sew from point D to point E.

chick, rear view

chick feet

7 Turn head upside down (head is right side out) and insert it into body, lining up points A and H. Pin head in place. Handstitch head to each side body from point A to point H and back to point A using tightly spaced stitches to make sure head is securely attached.

8 Machine sew between points H and E to finish sewing chick's body so that now there is an opening between the underbodies for turning and stuffing and an opening at the base of each leg for inserting the wire. Check all seams to make sure they are secure and reinforce any weak areas with additional stitching. Clip curves. Turn chick right side out, first pulling each leg into the body. Pull head out through opening and turn the rest of the body right side out. Use forceps to push the legs and tail out.

9 Stuff the chick with small pieces of stuffing, beginning at the head and working your way down, packing the stuffing very firmly as you go.

10 Pause when you are about ½" (1.3 cm) from the bottom of the chick to insert the 16-gauge wire. Insert the wire for the legs and feet.

11 Finish stuffing, pushing small bits of stuffing into the body to cover the wire and hold it in place. Push stuffing bit by bit into the leg openings and the tail. Push as much stuffing into the chick as possible.

12 Form the feet. The total length of the finished leg should be about 1" (2.5 cm). The total length of the longest toe should be about 1" (2.5 cm). Balance the bird.

13 Push a bit more stuffing into the body and close the opening with ladder stitch. Wrap the legs and feet with white floral tape. Mix white and yellow acrylic paint until you achieve a lemony yellow color and paint the floral tape. Seal with an acrylic sealer such as Mod Podge.

14 Match up one Wing of fur and one Wing of cotton fabric, right sides together, and stitch, leaving an opening for turning between point J and point K for turning. Repeat for other wing. Turn wings right side out through opening. Fold raw edges inward and sew opening closed with ladder stitch.

chick eye
+beak

15 Pin wings to chick. Stitch wings to body with ladder stitch or your preferred handstitch, sewing around the curved edges of each wing and leaving the back tips of the wings unattached.

16 Fold scrap of wool felt in half. Using Beak pattern, cut beak on the fold. Apply a thin coat of craft glue to the fold of the beak. Place beak on bird and pin in place with appliqué pins until glue dries.

17 Use pins to mark eye placement. Sew a bead at markings with black thread.

Swan

Swans are majestic birds; single or in pairs, these birds conjure ideas of love and fidelity. Because the swan's body is mostly white, I've added some embroidery stitches to break up the space and provide some visual interest. Silver eyelashes and lace feathers add romantic elegance. No wire is needed for this project; a smooth stone inserted into the body adds stability. This elegant fabric swan will add an air of beauty and romance wherever it is placed, and it makes a romantic gift.

FINISHED SIZE
8½" (21.5 cm) tall and 11" (28 cm) long

MATERIALS
White cotton fabric for body, wings, tail, and feathers, ¾ yd (68.5 cm)

Scraps of lace for feathers

Scrap of navy blue wool fabric for eye mask

Scrap of red cotton fabric for beak

Wool stuffing, 14 oz (397 g)

Embroidery floss in navy, black, silver, white, and cream

White and navy thread

Smooth round or oval stone for weight, about 1½" (3.8 cm) in diameter

TOOLS
Basic birdmaking tool kit

Clear tape

PATTERN PIECES
(pages 144–145)

Side Body and Head
(tape together,
cut 1, cut 1 reverse)

Bottom Gusset (cut 1)

Head Gusset (cut 1)

Mask (cut as directed)

Wing (cut 2, cut 2 reverse)

Tail (cut 2)

Beak (cut as directed)

NOTES
- Before you begin, read Basic Bird-making Techniques, pages 19–39, for detailed instructions on the birdmaking process.
- Add ¼" (6 mm) seam allowance to all pattern pieces except where noted.

1 Prewash and iron all fabrics. Trace pattern pieces onto freezer paper and cut out. Attach Head pattern piece to Side Body pattern piece with clear tape. Be sure to trace left and right versions of the combined Side Body/Head and the Wing.

2 Iron freezer paper pattern pieces to fabric, matte side up, and cut left and right Side Body pieces, one Head Gusset, and one Bottom Gusset from white cotton fabric (use a scrap of fabric as a press cloth over tape to prevent it from melting). Transfer all markings.

3 Sew one long edge of Bottom Gusset to bottom of one Side Body from point A to point B. Sew the other long edge of the Bottom Gusset to the other Side Body the same way.

4 Sew Head Gusset to one Side Body from point C to point D. Sew Head Gusset to other Side Body the same way.

5 Stitch around remainder of swan from point A, along the swan's back, to point C and from point D, down the swan's neck, to point B. Swan is now sewn completely.

6 Clip all curves. Check seams and reinforce as needed.

7 Using small, sharp scissors, make a 1½" (3.8 cm) slit in the bottom gusset parallel to stitching lines. Insert forceps into slit. Pull swan's tail into its body. Grasp swan's head and

swan mask
sewn to head
with navy
blue stitches

pull it out through the slit. Pull remainder of body out through the slit so that swan is now right side out.

8 Stuff the swan with small pieces of stuffing, reaching forceps into the body through the slit. Begin at the head and work your way down, packing the stuffing very firmly as you go. Pay particular attention to the swan's neck to make sure it is firmly stuffed and not lumpy.

9 About ¼" (6 mm) from the bottom of the swan's body, pause to insert a smooth stone. Keep stone flat and parallel with bottom gusset. Push stuffing around stone so that it is firmly in place and is cushioned. Finish stuffing swan.

10 Mold swan's body with your hands to make sure it is balanced. Adjust stuffing or stone as needed. Turn raw edges of slit inward. Close the opening with a neat ladder stitch or your preferred handstitch.

11 Using Wing and Tail pattern pieces, make two wing bases and one tail base.

12 Create rows of looped feathers from torn strips of body fabric interspersed with strips cut from lace **(figs. 1 and 2)**.

13 Pin tail to swan with top of the tail on swan's body and bottom extending about 1" (2.5 cm) past end of swan body. Tack down with a few handstitches. Pin wings to swan. Tack down.

fig. 1: first row of feathers on outer edge of wing.

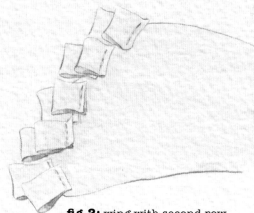

fig.2: wing with second row of feathers sewn.

swan eye,
mask +
beak

17 With two strands of white embroidery floss, make small straight stitches at base of swan's neck. Continue to densely stitch neck with white and cream floss until a feathery look is achieved.

14 Iron Eye Mask pattern piece to navy blue wool. Cut around pattern piece exactly (do not add seam allowance). Pull off pattern piece. Lay mask on swan's face, making sure it is symmetrically placed. Pin using appliqué pins. Handstitch mask to swan with navy blue thread and long straight visible stitches.

15 Iron Beak pattern piece, matte side up, to a double layer of red cotton fabric, right sides together. Sew directly around the freezer paper, leaving base of beak open. Trim close to stitching. Turn beak right side out, turn raw edge under and baste, stuff beak, and pin to bird. Stitch to head through mask using ladder stitch.

16 Draw eyes with disappearing ink fabric marker. With two strands of navy embroidery floss, embroider eyes with satin stitch. Outline eyes with a single strand of black floss using running stitch or backstitch. Satin-stitch eyeballs with a single strand of black floss over navy blue eyes. With a single strand of silver floss, make three eyelashes at the edge of each eye with straight stitches (for stitches, see page 137).

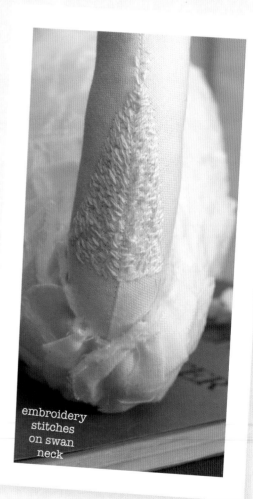

embroidery
stitches
on swan
neck

ASSEMBLAGE ON STRETCHED CANVAS OR WOOD

Influenced by work like Joseph Cornell's aviary shadow boxes, I love to join my interest in collage and my love of sewing fabric birds by making three-dimensional assemblages with birds. To enhance the three-dimensional feel, I then add some found objects, bits of fabric, and thread. Creating an assemblage is an inventive way to display a fabric bird on a wall instead of on a shelf. To create your own unique bird assemblage, follow these steps:

1 Find a support such as a wooden board, a stretched canvas, or a shadow box.

2 Choose some paper ephemera and arrange it in a pleasing composition on the support. Cover the support in acrylic sealer, such as Mod Podge, and then glue the papers down. Do not dip your brush in water or the papers will bubble. If any bubbles do form, smooth them out with your fingertips as you work. Cover the papers with more acrylic sealer and add more papers until you feel the collage is finished.

3 Sew a bird in a color palette that coordinates with your collage. The lark and wren are both small birds that work well in assemblages, but any bird pattern can be reduced to 75 percent of its original size (or less) and made small enough to incorporate into a composition.

4 Now go back to the collage and glue down some fabric scraps, threads, and other small found objects with craft glue. Affix the bird to a perch with two-part epoxy. Let the glue dry completely and then affix the perch to the collage with a combination of nails and epoxy so that it is firmly in place and can support the weight of the bird.

Woodpecker

This project began with a walk in the woods with my daughters. We found a piece of tree bark with a perfectly oval hole that had clearly been created by a woodpecker. I brought it home and hung the bark on the wall—and then I just had to make a woodpecker to perch on it. Of all of the birds I've made, the woodpecker most closely resembles the real thing, with its black and white plumage, bright red crest, and long pointed beak. Take a nature walk and find an interesting piece of bark or branch that could serve as a perch, and then get started making this woodpecker.

FINISHED SIZE

Bark, as shown, 18" × 4" (45.5 x 10 cm) at widest point; bird, 7¼" × 3¼" (18.5 × 8.5 cm)

MATERIALS

White fabric for body, wings, and tail, ¼ yd (23 cm)

Scrap of red fabric for crest

Scraps of black and black-and-white print fabric for feathers

Wool stuffing, 10 oz (283 g)

Dark brown embroidery floss

White thread

Dark brown floral tape

16-gauge brass wire, 36" (91.5 cm)

20-gauge aluminum wire, 14" (35.5 cm), and 2 small nails to hang finished piece

Dark brown polymer clay (one package is enough for several beaks)

Plank of wood or tree branch

TOOLS

Basic birdmaking tool kit

Two-part epoxy adhesive

Popsicle stick for mixing epoxy adhesive

Hammer

PATTERN PIECES (page 143)

Side Body (cut 1, cut 1 reverse)

Underbody (cut 1, cut 1 reverse)

Head Gusset (cut 1)

Crest (cut as directed)

Stripe (cut 1 on fold)

Wing (cut 2, cut 2 reverse)

Tail (cut 2)

Beak (cut as directed)

NOTES

● Before you begin, read Basic Birdmaking Techniques, pages 19–39, for detailed instructions on the birdmaking process.

● Add ¼" (6 mm) seam allowance to all pattern pieces except where noted.

1 Prewash and iron all fabrics. Trace pattern pieces onto freezer paper and cut out. Be sure to cut left and right versions of Side Body, Underbody, and Wing.

2 Iron freezer paper pattern pieces to fabric, matte side up, and cut left and right Side Body, left and right Underbody, and Head Gusset from bird body fabric. Transfer all markings.

3 Pin Underbody pieces, right sides together, along top edge. Stitch along the top edge, from point A to point B and from point C to point D, leaving a 1" (2.5 cm) opening in the center of the seam for turning and stuffing.

4 Pin one Underbody to one Side Body, right sides together. Stitch along the bottom of the bird, leaving an opening at the base of the leg for inserting wire. Repeat with other Underbody and Side Body so that the bottom of the woodpecker is now sewn.

5 Pin Head Gusset to top of head area on one Side Body, right sides together. Sew from point E to point F. Pin other side of Head Gusset to other Side Body and sew from point E to point F.

6 Sew remaining body seams (from point A to point F and then from point E to point D) so that now the woodpecker's body is sewn completely, with an opening for turning and stuffing on the underbody seam and an opening at the base of each leg for inserting the wire.

7 Clip all curves, especially near the legs. Reinforce seams as needed. Use forceps to gently pull the legs into the body, then the tail, and finally the head. Gently turn the woodpecker right side out through the opening left in the underbody seam, pulling the head through the opening first. Use forceps to push the legs and tail out. Stuff the woodpecker with small pieces of stuffing, beginning at the head and working your way down, packing the stuffing very firmly as you go.

8 When you have about ½" (1.3 cm) remaining to be stuffed at the bottom of the woodpecker, pause to insert the 16-gauge wire.

9 Finish stuffing, pushing small bits of stuffing into the body to cover the wire and hold it in place. Push stuffing bit by bit into the leg openings and the tail. Push as much stuffing into the woodpecker as possible.

10 Form the feet with the wire. The total length of each finished leg should be about ½" (1.3 cm). The total length of the longest toe should be about ½" (1.3 cm). Don't be concerned with balancing the woodpecker because later its legs will be pushed forward and its feet bent around the wood it will stand on.

11 Push a bit more stuffing into the bird's body and close the opening with ladder stitch. Wrap the legs and feet with floral tape. Bend the legs so that the woodpecker is parallel with the piece of wood that it will stand on. Bend the toes so that they will rest flush against the wood when glued.

woodpecker
crest, stripe
+ beak

woodpecker
stripe,
rear view

woodpecker
feet on
wood base

TIP
polymer clay is
perfect for shaping
the woodpecker's
sharp beak

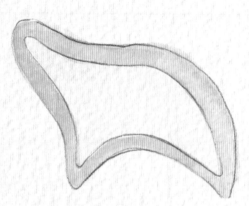

fig. 1: iron Crest freezer paper pattern piece to fabric.

fig. 2: stuffed crest is pinned and ready to be handsewn to woodpecker's head.

12 Iron the Crest pattern piece to the wrong side of the scrap of red fabric **(fig. 1)**. Place the scrap against a second scrap of red fabric, right sides together. With pattern piece still adhered to fabric, machine stitch around pattern, leaving base open for turning and stuffing. Trim around pattern piece ⅛" (3 mm) from seam line. Pull pattern piece off. Turn crest right side out using forceps. Fold raw edges inward and baste. Stuff crest using tiny amounts of stuffing at a time. Pin crest to woodpecker's head using appliqué pins **(fig. 2)**. Stitch crest to head with ladder stitch or your preferred handstitch.

13 Iron the Stripe pattern piece to a folded scrap of black fabric. Cut out directly around pattern piece. Pull off pattern piece. Cut almost, but not completely, through fold, so the two pieces of the stripe are still connected by a few threads, as shown in the photograph on page 77, upper right. Apply a thin layer of craft glue to wrong side of stripe. Press stripe onto woodpecker's head. Hold in place with appliqué pins while glue dries.

14 Draw eyes with disappearing ink fabric marker. Using two strands of brown embroidery floss, embroider the eyeballs with satin stitch and eyelashes with stem stitch (see page 137).

15 Using Wing and Tail pattern pieces, cut and sew bases for the wings and the tail. Sew rows of looped feathers in black for the tail and in a black-and-white print for the wings.

16 Pin tail to bird and tack down with a few ladder stitches or your preferred handstitch. Pin wings to the woodpecker's back and tack down.

17 Pinch off a small amount of dark brown polymer clay and knead it to warm it up and make it pliable. Roll it against the work surface to create a tapered cone with one pointed end and one blunt end. Bake according to package directions. Cool completely. Apply a small amount of craft glue to the blunt end of beak. Press to woodpecker's face and hold in place until the glue is dry enough to bond securely. Let glue dry completely.

18 Following safety precautions for epoxy adhesive, mix a small amount of two-part epoxy with a popsicle stick. Apply a coating of epoxy to the underside of the woodpecker's feet and press onto your bark or wood. Prop up woodpecker until glue dries completely.

19 To ready the finished sculpture for hanging, turn the piece of bark or wooden base over to the back. Being careful of the woodpecker on the other side, gently tap a small nail about halfway into either side of the wood. Wind the length of 20-gauge aluminum wire around one nail, across the wood to the other nail, and around the other nail. Trim off excess wire. Tap nails further into wood.

Penguin

The penguin is a flightless bird with smooth wings that are almost like flippers. Penguins spend almost half their lives underwater. On the ice, they're either waddling or hopping on short legs or sliding on their bellies. With tuxedo coloration, an endearing waddle, and general friendliness to humans, the penguin is a universal favorite bird species, and a handmade fabric penguin will be admired and adored wherever it resides. If you like, make a fabric egg and place it on the penguin's feet.

FINISHED SIZE
11½" (29 cm) tall

MATERIALS
White cotton fabric for body, ¼ yd (23 cm)

Black cotton fabric for body and top of wings, ½ yd (45.5 cm)

Gray fabric for beak, underside of wings, and wrapping legs, ⅛ yd (11.5 cm)

Scrap of yellow fabric for beak

Stuffing, 20 oz (567 g)

16-gauge brass wire, 24" (51 cm)

Dark brown floral tape

White, black, and gray embroidery floss

TOOLS
Basic birdmaking tool kit

Fabric chalk or white fabric pencil

Clear tape

PATTERN PIECES
(pages 146–147)

Side Body (tape A + B together and cut 1, cut 1 reverse)

Underbody (cut 1, cut 1 reverse)

Head Gusset (cut 1)

Back Gusset (cut 1)

Wing (from gray fabric, cut 1, cut 1 reverse; from black fabric, cut 1, cut 1 reverse)

Beak (cut as directed)

Beak Gusset (cut 1)

NOTES
● Before you begin, read through chapter 2, Basic Birdmaking Techniques, pages 19–39, for detailed instructions on the birdmaking process.

● Add ¼" (6 mm) seam allowance to all pattern pieces except where noted.

1 Prewash and iron all fabrics. Trace pattern pieces onto freezer paper and cut out. Attach Side Body pattern pieces together with clear tape. Be sure to cut right and left versions of Side Body, Underbody, and Wing.

2 Iron freezer paper pattern pieces to fabric, matte side up, and cut left and right Side Body pieces, Head Gusset, and Back Gusset from black fabric (use a scrap of fabric as a press cloth over tape to prevent it from melting). Cut left and right Underbody pieces from white fabric. Transfer all markings.

3 Pin Underbody pieces, right sides together, from point A to point B. Stitch. Pin oval leg dart on underbody and stitch dart.

4 After Underbodies are attached, make a pleat in excess fabric near top of underbody, and slip-stitch this pleat closed to create a smooth underbody that does not have wrinkles when stuffed.

5 Pin the Back Gusset to one Side Body from point G to point H. Stitch. Repeat for other Side Body.

6 Pin the Head Gusset to one Side Body from point E to point F. Stitch. Repeat for the other Side Body.

7 Pin the Underbody to one Side Body from point C to point B and sew. Repeat for the other Side Body.

8 Continue sewing around remainder of penguin, from point G to point E, from point F to point B. Sew from point H to point C, leaving an opening at the base of the leg for inserting the leg wire and leaving an opening underneath the tail for turning and stuffing.

penguin
legs + feet

9 Clip curves. Check all seams and reinforce with additional stitching as needed.

10 Use forceps to gently turn penguin right side out through opening underneath the tail. Stuff penguin very firmly. This bird requires a lot of stuffing and takes a good bit of time to stuff properly.

11 When you have about ½" (1.3 cm) remaining to be stuffed, pause to insert the 16-gauge wire.

12 After inserting wire, finish stuffing, pushing small bits of stuffing into the body to cover the wire and hold it in place. Push stuffing bit by bit into the leg openings and the tail. Stuff the bird very firmly.

13 Form the feet with the wire. The length of the finished leg should be about ¾" (2 cm). The length of the longest toe should be about 1" (2.5 cm). Balance the bird.

14 Push a bit more stuffing into the body and close the opening with ladder stitch using black thread. Wrap the legs and feet tightly with floral tape. Wrap again with torn strips of gray fabric, leaving the toenails exposed. Wrap again with black thread if desired.

15 Using the Beak pattern piece, cut two beak pieces from gray fabric. Cut one Beak Gusset piece from yellow fabric.

penguin wing,
showing
contrasting
underside

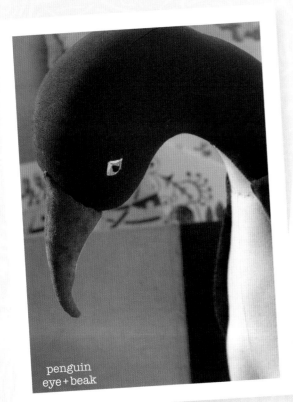

penguin
eye + beak

penguin,
rear view

16 Pin Beak Gusset to one Beak piece, right sides facing, and stitch along Beak Gusset from point I1 to point J. Repeat with second Beak piece, sewing from I2 to J, so that now the gusset is fully attached. Sew the two Beak pieces together on remaining edge, leaving the base of the beak open for turning and stuffing. Trim seam allowances to within ⅛" (3 mm). Turn beak right side out using forceps **(fig. 1)**. Turn raw edge under and baste. Stuff beak firmly by pushing tiny bits of stuffing at a time all the way to the tip of the beak. Pin beak to penguin and attach with ladder stitch or your preferred handstitch.

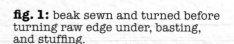

fig. 1: beak sewn and turned before turning raw edge under, basting, and stuffing.

17 Cut a Wing from black fabric and a Wing from gray fabric. Match up the two Wing pieces, right sides together, and stitch around, leaving an opening for turning. Use forceps to turn wing right side out. Turn raw edges at opening inward and press. Stitch opening closed with ladder stitch using black thread. Repeat for other wing, being sure to reverse the pattern piece so that you create two wings that are mirror images of one another. Pin wings to penguin. Attach along the top curve and extending 1" (2.5 cm) down on each side, using ladder stitch or your preferred handstitch. Repeat for other wing.

18 With fabric chalk or white fabric pencil, sketch eye onto penguin. Using satin stitch (see page 137), use two strands of white embroidery floss to embroider whites of eyes, two strands of black embroidery floss for eyeballs, and two strands of gray floss for lower lid.

penguin, side view

Owl

When I bring friends up to my studio, they are always drawn to the owls; I think it's the large forward-facing eyes that attract their attention. Because it's rare to see an owl in the wild—most owls are nocturnal and are well camouflaged with their natural environment—it might also be a little thrilling to be close to a fabric owl. This is one of my favorite projects; large wings and a long tail provide room to play with colors, patterns, and textures. This pattern allows you to make an owl with its head turned in any direction just as in real life. A completed owl is a showpiece!

FINISHED SIZE
12½" (31.5 cm) tall to top of ear

MATERIALS
Fabric for bird body, ½ yd (45.5 cm)

3 different fabrics for feathers, beak, eyes, ears, and other details, ¼ yd (23 cm) of each

Wool stuffing, 14 oz (397 g)

16-gauge brass wire, 36" (91.5 cm)

Black or brown floral tape

Black, white, and brown embroidery floss

TOOLS
Basic birdmaking tool kit

PATTERN PIECES
(pages 150–151)

Side Body (cut 1, cut 1 reverse)

Underbody (cut 1, cut 1 reverse)

Head (cut 2)

Head Gusset (cut 1)

Back Gusset (cut 1)

Tail (cut 2)

Wing (cut 2, cut 2 reverse)

Eye Base (cut as directed)

Middle Eye Layer (cut as directed)

Top Eye Layer (cut as directed)

Ear (cut as directed)

Beak (cut as directed)

NOTES
◆ Before you begin, read Basic Birdmaking Techniques, pages 19–39, for detailed instructions on the birdmaking process.

◆ Add ¼" (6 mm) seam allowance to all pattern pieces except where noted.

owl legs + feet

owl wings from the side

1 Prewash and iron all fabrics. Trace pattern pieces onto freezer paper and cut out. Be sure to cut left and right versions of Side Body, Underbody, and Wing.

2 Iron freezer paper pattern pieces to fabric, matte side up, and cut left and right Side Body pieces, left and right Underbody pieces, two Head pieces, one Back Gusset, and one Head Gusset from bird body fabric. Transfer all markings.

3 Make an oval dart on each Underbody piece. To make dart, fold leg up at straight line, pin, and stitch along dotted line. Repeat on the other Underbody. Fold leg on each Underbody back down and pin or baste dart to leg to keep flat.

4 Pin Underbody pieces, right sides together, along top edge. Stitch from point A to point B and from point C to point D, leaving a 1" (2.5 cm) opening in the center of the seam for turning and stuffing.

5 Pin one long edge of Back Gusset to one Side Body, right sides together, matching markings. Stitch from point E to the tip of the gusset at point F. Pin the other edge of Back Gusset to the second Side Body, stitching from point E to point F.

6 Pin one Underbody to one Side Body, right sides together, pinning from leg to the tip of Underbody at point D. Stitch, leaving an opening at the base of the leg for inserting the wire. Pin the other edge of that same Underbody to Side Body, stitching from leg to the tip of the Underbody at point B, removing pins as you go. The fold of the dart can point up or down, but I usually like it pointing up. Repeat with the other Underbody and Side Body so that the bottom of the owl is now sewn.

7 Beginning at the breast at point B, sew up to the top of the owl's body. Beginning at the top of the back part of the underbody, sew up to the tip of the back gusset at point F so that now the owl's body is fully sewn, with an opening for the head and an opening for stuffing and turning on underbody seam.

8 Stitch the three darts on each Head piece. Align the center of one long edge of Head Gusset with the top dart on one Head piece, right sides together. Pin Head Gusset to outer edge of Head and stitch seam, stitching from top center to bottom edge on one side and repeating on the other side. Pin the remaining long edge of Head Gusset to the other Head piece and repeat. Clip curves and turn the head right side out.

9 Insert head inside the owl body, right sides together. Match and pin raw edges together. To turn the owl's head, shift it a few inches to the right or left and pin as desired. Stitch seam.

10 Clip all curves, especially near the legs. Use forceps to gently pull the legs into the body, then the tail. Gently turn the owl right side out through the opening left in the underbody seam, pulling the head through the opening first. Use the forceps to push the legs and tail out. Stuff the owl with small pieces of stuffing, beginning at the head and working your way down, packing the stuffing very firmly as you go.

owl wings + tail, rear view

owl tail + wings with stitching showing underneath

13 Wrap the legs and feet with torn strips of fabric and thread, leaving the talons exposed.

14 Use the Wing pattern piece to make two wing bases from main bird body fabric and use the Tail pattern piece to make a tail base from bird body fabric. Cover the wings and tail with feathers made from loops of torn fabric strips, using the different-colored additional fabrics.

15 Pin tail to stuffed owl body and tack down with a strong thread and a heavy needle, using ladder stitch or your preferred handstitch. Pin wings to owl body and tack down in the same manner. Rebalance the bird.

16 Iron Beak pattern piece, matte side up, to a double layer of beak fabric, right sides together. Stitch around the perimeter of the pattern piece, leaving the base of the beak open. Pull off freezer paper and trim the beak close to stitching. Turn beak right side out, turn raw edge under, baste, and stuff. Set aside.

11 When you have about ½" (1.3 cm) of the owl remaining to stuff, pause to insert the wire and make the feet. Finish stuffing, pushing small bits of stuffing into the body to cover the wire and hold it in place. Push stuffing bit by bit into the leg openings and the tail. Stuff the owl as firmly as possible.

12 Shape the legs and feet. Legs should be about 2½" (6.5 cm) long, and the long center toe should be about 1" (2.5 cm) long. Balance the bird. Add more stuffing until you're satisfied with the firmness of the bird and close the opening with ladder stitch. Wrap the legs and feet tightly with floral tape for added stability.

17 Iron the eye pattern pieces Eye Base, Middle Eye Layer, and Top Eye Layer to double layers of scraps of fabric with wrong sides together (eyes are not turned), choosing different colors for the base, middle, and top eye pieces. A light-colored fabric is best for the Top Eye Layer. For each eye layer, machine stitch around the pattern pieces through both layers of fabric, trim shape ⅛" (3 mm) or less from stitching, and remove pattern piece. The eyes have raw edges and are not turned. Repeat once with the Top Eye layer and the Middle Eye layer so you have two of each.

18 Using a disappearing ink fabric marker, draw eyes onto Top Eye Layer. With two strands of embroidery floss, use satin stitch to embroider the eyeballs in black, whites of the eyes in white, and eyelids in brown. Stack the top, middle, and base layers of the eyes and join all layers together with a few ladder stitches or your preferred handstitch.

19 Pin the beak between the embroidered eyes and stitch beak to eye base firmly using ladder stitch or your preferred handstitch. Remove the basting stitches on the beak. Pin the eye base to the owl. Tack down around the inner parts of the eyes, leaving the outer parts unattached.

20 Iron the Ear pattern to the wrong side of a scrap of light-colored fabric. Place this fabric on top of the right side of a scrap of darker fabric, right sides together. Machine stitch around the ear from point G to point H, leaving the base (short straight edge) open for turning. Trim close to stitching. Pull pattern piece off. Use forceps to grasp the tip of the ear and turn it gently right side out. Fold the raw edge under and press. Fold the bottom left corner of the ear inward to the center and then the bottom right inward to the center, overlapping slightly, and pin. Make second ear, overlapping left corner over right. Using ladder stitch or your preferred handstitch, stitch ears to head gusset of owl, placing each one about 1½" (3.8 cm) from center top of owl's head.

owl eyes + ears

owl ear, side view

raptor

This raptor is a quirky little bird. He could be gearing up for a trans-Atlantic flight with his exaggerated head, aviator-style cap, and serious, determined expression. This bird is all about playing with form, fabric, and expression, so have fun with it. If the finished bird makes you laugh, you've done a great job.

FINISHED SIZE
10" (25.5 cm) tall

MATERIALS
Cream-colored cotton for bird body, ¼ yd (23 cm)

3 different-colored fabrics for details and feathers, ¼ yd (23 cm) of each

Wool stuffing, 10 oz (283 g)

16-gauge brass wire, 24" (61 cm)

Dark brown floral tape

Contrasting thread

Double-sided fusible web, ¼ yd (23 cm)

Dark brown or black embroidery floss

TOOLS
Basic birdmaking tool kit

OPTIONAL: Paddle punch in leaf shape, cutting mat or stack of old newspapers, and hammer

PATTERN PIECES
(pages 148 and 152)

Side Body (cut 1, cut 1 reverse)

Underbody (cut 1, cut 1 reverse)

Head (cut 1, cut 1 reverse)

Head Gusset (cut 1)

Cap (cut 1)

Wing (cut 2, cut 2 reverse)

Tail (cut 2)

Eye Mask (cut as directed)

Beak (cut as directed)

NOTES
● Before you begin, read Basic Birdmaking Techniques, pages 19–39, for detailed instructions on the birdmaking process.

● Add ¼" (6 mm) seam allowance to all pattern pieces except where noted.

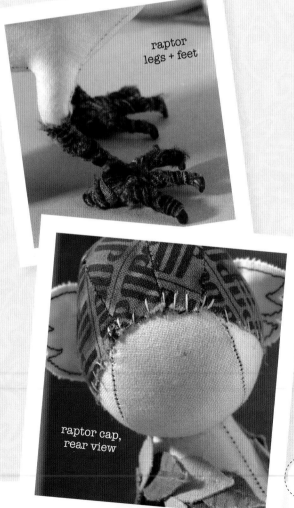

1 Prewash and iron all fabrics. Trace patterns onto freezer paper and cut out. Be sure to cut left and right versions of Side Body, Underbody, Wing, and Eye Mask.

2 Iron freezer paper patterns onto fabric, matte side up, and cut left and right Side Body, left and right Underbody, two Head pieces, and one Head Gusset piece from cream-colored cotton fabric. Transfer all markings.

3 Sew oval-shaped darts at the top of each Underbody leg. Fold leg down and pin down to keep it out of the way while you do the next step.

4 Pin Underbody pieces, right sides together, along top edge. Stitch across top edge from point A to point B and from point C to point D, leaving a 1" (2.5 cm) opening in the center of the seam for turning and stuffing.

5 Pin one Underbody to one Side Body, right sides together, with the dart pointed upward. Stitch along bottom of the bird, leaving an opening at the base of each leg for inserting the wire. Repeat with other Underbody and Side Body so that the bottom of the raptor's body is now sewn.

6 Continue sewing around the rest of the body from point A around the neck to point D so that the entire body is now sewn, with an opening between the underbodies for turning and stuffing, and openings at the base of each leg for inserting the wire.

7 Clip curves. Reinforce seams as needed. Use forceps to turn the bird, pulling the legs and neck into the body and then pulling the rest of the body right side out.

8 Stuff the raptor firmly. When you have about ½" (1.3 cm) remaining to be stuffed, pause to insert the 16-gauge wire. Finish stuffing, pushing small bits of stuffing into the body to cover the wire and hold it in place. Add stuffing bit by bit into the leg opening and the tail. Push as much stuffing into the bird as possible.

9 Form legs and feet. Legs should be 1½" (3.8 cm) long and toes should be 1" (2.5 cm) long. Balance the bird. Push a bit more stuffing into body and close opening with ladder stitch or your preferred handstitch.

raptor legs + feet

raptor cap, rear view

10 Wrap legs and feet tightly with floral tape. Wrap legs and feet with torn strips of fabric and again with contrasting thread, leaving the talons exposed. Set body aside.

11 To sew the head, line up the bottom of one Head piece with the straight edge of the Head Gusset, matching points E and E1. Slowly stitch the side of the Gusset to the Head, matching points F and F1, easing the edges as you sew around and leaving the bottom unstitched. Repeat for the other Head piece, matching points E and E2 and sewing to F, leaving the bottom open for turning and stuffing. Clip all curves. Turn the head right side out. Turn the raw edges under and baste. Firmly stuff the head, leaving a little room at the bottom for inserting the neck of the bird body.

12 Put the head onto the neck and pin all the way around, adding bits of stuffing as needed. The raptor's head can be looking straight ahead or can be turned or tilted in any direction. Stitch the head to the neck using small ladder stitches or your preferred handstitch **(fig. 1)**. Pull out the basting stitches. Rebalance the bird.

13 Iron the Cap pattern piece to a single layer of patterned scrap fabric. Cut out exactly around the pattern piece, leaving no seam allowance **(fig. 2)**. Transfer dart markings. Snip and sew all three darts **(fig. 3)**.

14 Put a wad of stuffing inside cap to fill it almost completely and pin cap to bird's head **(fig. 4)**. Using a contrasting thread and long visible stitches, handstitch cap to head, leaving about 1" (2.5 cm) open at the back to push in more stuffing. Stretch and ease cap to fit snugly around the head. Finish stitching the cap to the head.

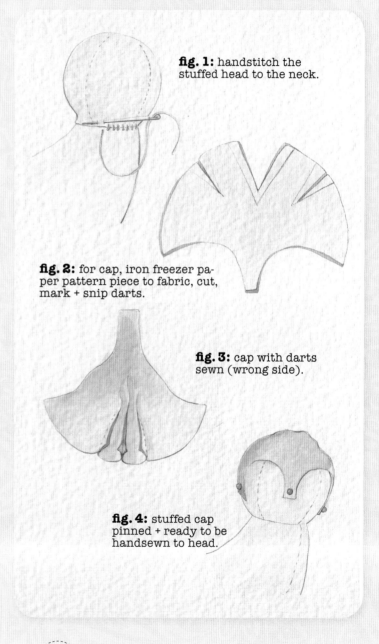

fig. 1: handstitch the stuffed head to the neck.

fig. 2: for cap, iron freezer paper pattern piece to fabric, cut, mark + snip darts.

fig. 3: cap with darts sewn (wrong side).

fig. 4: stuffed cap pinned + ready to be handsewn to head.

raptor
wings + tail,
back view

raptor eye
mask

15 Using Wing and Tail pattern pieces, make two wing bases and one tail base.

16 Make punched feathers as described for the Lark, page 54, steps 19 and 20. You will need three or four sheets of fused fabric, each a different color, to cut or punch enough feathers for this bird.

17 Spray one side of both wing bases and tail base with a light coating of spray adhesive. Beginning at the tip of the tail and the tips of the wings, place a feather and stitch down with one or two handstitches at the top of the feather. For the second row, place two feathers overlapping the top of the first row and handstitch each one down. Continue this way, covering both wings and the tail with handstitched feathers. Pin the tail onto the body and tack down with handstitches. Pin wings onto body and tack down.

18 Iron the Eye Mask pattern piece to a double layer of scraps, wrong sides together (eye mask is not turned), of the cream-colored fabric. Machine stitch around pattern piece. Pull off pattern piece. Trim ⅛" (3 mm) from stitching line. Repeat for second Eye Mask.

19 Draw eyeball and brow with disappearing ink fabric marker. Using two strands of embroidery floss, embroider the eyes, using one long straight stitch for the brow and satin stitch for the eyeball (see page 137). Pin the eye mask to the bird and tack down.

20 Iron the Beak pattern piece to a double layer of fabric, rights sides together. Stitch around edge of freezer paper, leaving base of beak open. Trim close to stitching. Pull pattern piece off. Turn beak right side out, turn under raw edges and baste, stuff beak, and sew to bird with ladder stitch or your preferred handstitch.

USING FOUND FABRICS

I love to create something from noth-
ing, and I especially love transforming something that's been discarded
as trash into a marvelous treasure of
a bird. Fabric bits come into our lives
without us even noticing and go out
of our lives in the trash just as unno-
ticed—how, I've wondered, can I work
with those fabrics? One day, I cut all
the labels out of my clothing and pieced
them together, and then made a little
lark with clothing label wings.

I've experimented with other found
fabrics. I've cut up bar towels and
made them into raptors and sewn
birds from flour sacks. The printed
text on all of these fabrics gets ob-
scured when they are cut and sewn
together; the juxtaposition makes the
viewer come in for a closer look and
maybe think twice about throwing out
fabrics that are used to hold and label
the things we own.

Always keep an eye out for found
fabrics that you can integrate into
your own birdmaking, and you'll find
that they add interest and character
to your birds.

wading bird

The first fabric bird I ever made was a wading bird. I went on to make six more as part of a display I was creating at our local public library, where I arranged the birds amid dry reeds with dim lighting, as if they were taxidermy specimens in an old natural history museum. I had more than fifty soft sculptures set up throughout the library, but the wading birds attracted the most attention, so they hold a special place in my heart. This bird is somewhat complex to construct and balance; patiently tweaking the legs and toes and making them with a strong wire bound tightly with floral tape is the key to success.

FINISHED SIZE
15½" (39.5 cm) tall

MATERIALS
Light-colored fabric for body, wings, and tail, ½ yd (45.5 cm)

3 different cotton fabrics for feathers, ¼ yd (23 cm) of each

Scrap of brown fabric for beak

Scrap of yellow fabric for crest

Wool stuffing, 14 oz (397 g)

16-gauge brass wire, 48" (122 cm)

Dark brown floral tape

Brown embroidery floss

Lightweight fusible interfacing, ⅛ yd (10 cm)

TOOLS
Basic birdmaking tool kit

Clear tape

PATTERN PIECES
(pages 148–149)

Side Body and Head (tape together two parts and cut 1, cut 1 reverse)

Underbody (cut 1, cut 1 reverse)

Head Gusset (cut 1)

Beak (cut as directed)

Tail (cut 2)

Wing (cut 2, cut 2 reverse)

Crest (cut as directed)

NOTES
- Before you begin, read Basic Birdmaking Techniques, pages 19–39, for detailed instructions on the birdmaking process.
- Add ¼" (6 mm) seam allowance to all pattern pieces except where noted.

1 Prewash and iron all fabrics. Trace pattern pieces onto freezer paper and cut out. Be sure to cut left and right versions of Side Body, Head, Underbody, and Wing. Attach Head pattern piece to Side Body pattern piece with tape.

2 Iron freezer paper pattern pieces to fabric, matte side up, and cut left and right Side Body pieces, left and right Underbody pieces, and one Head Gusset from body fabric (use a scrap of fabric as a press cloth when ironing over tape to prevent melting). Transfer all markings.

3 Stitch oval darts at the top of each Underbody. Fold legs down and pin down to keep them out of the way while you stitch the next step.

4 Pin Underbody pieces, right sides together, along top edge. Stitch along the top edge from point A to point B and from point C to point D, leaving a 1" (2.5 cm) opening in the center of the seam for turning and stuffing.

5 Pin one Underbody to one Side Body, right sides together, with the dart pointed upward. Stitch along the bottom of the bird, leaving an opening at the base of the leg for inserting the wire. Repeat with other Underbody and Side Body so that the bottom of the wading bird is now sewn.

6 Pin Head Gusset to one Side Body, right sides together. Sew from point E to point F. Pin other Head Gusset to other Side Body and sew from point E to point F.

wading bird legs + feet

7 Sew remaining body seams (from point A to point F and then from point E to point D) so that now the wading bird's body is sewn completely, with an opening for turning and stuffing on the underbody seam and openings at the base of each leg for inserting the wire.

wading bird
upper legs
+ underbody

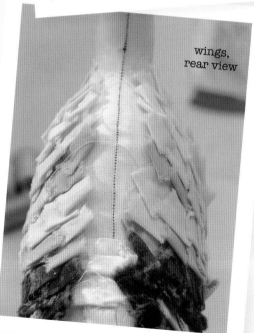

wings,
rear view

8 Clip all curves, especially near the leg openings. Reinforce seams with additional stitching if needed. Using forceps, gently turn the wading bird right side out through the opening left in the underbody seam, pulling the legs into the body, then the tail, and finally the head. Use forceps to push the legs and tail out. Stuff the wading bird with small pieces of stuffing, beginning at the head and working your way down. Pay particular attention to stuffing the neck smoothly and firmly to avoid any lumps or understuffed areas.

9 When you have about ½" (1.3 cm) remaining to be stuffed at the bottom of the wading bird, pause and insert the 16-gauge wire.

10 Finish stuffing, pushing small bits of stuffing into the body to cover the wire and hold it in place. Push stuffing bit by bit into the leg openings and the tail end of the bird. Push as much stuffing into the wading bird as possible.

11 Form the feet. The total length of each finished leg should be about 5" (12.5 cm). The total length of the longest toe on each foot should be about 1½" (3.8 cm). Legs any longer than 5" (12.5 cm) will make it very difficult to balance the bird.

101

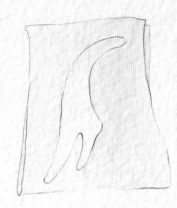

fig. 1: crest freezer paper pattern on a double layer of yellow fabric, right sides together.

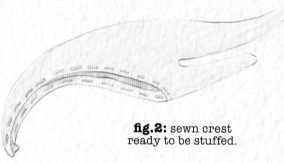

fig.2: sewn crest ready to be stuffed.

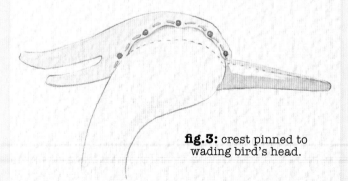

fig.3: crest pinned to wading bird's head.

12 To balance the bird, stand the bird up and place one hand on top of the bird's feet. Hold the feet firmly down on the work surface. With the other hand adjust the legs and the position of the body. Slight adjustments make a big difference. Continue to bend the wire ever so slightly until the bird balances on its own.

13 Push a bit more stuffing into the body and close the opening with ladder stitch. Wrap the legs and feet very tightly with floral tape. For this bird, stability is key. The tighter the legs are wrapped, particularly at the top where the wire meets the fabric of the legs and down where each toe meets the base of the foot, the more stable the bird will be. You may want to wrap the legs a second or third time to add some thickness to the wire and to provide further stability.

14 Using the Wing pattern piece, sew wing bases. Using the three different cotton fabrics, sew rows of looped feathers to the wings.

15 Sew a tail base using the Tail pattern piece, sandwiching a piece of lightweight interfacing between the layers to hold the weight of the tail and prevent it from drooping when attached to the bird. Sew rows of looped feathers in various colors to the tail.

16 Pin tail to bird and tack down with a few ladder stitches or your preferred handstitch.

wading bird
head + eye
details

wading
bird tail

17 Pin wings to the back of the bird and tack down.

18 Iron Beak pattern piece to a double layer of fabric, right sides together. Stitch around edge of freezer paper, leaving base open. Trim fabric close to stitching and along lower edge. Pull pattern piece off. Turn beak, turn raw edges under and baste, stuff beak, and attach to bird with ladder stitch or your preferred handstitch.

19 Iron the Crest pattern piece to a double layer of yellow fabric, right sides together **(fig. 1)**. Stitch around the edge of the pattern piece, leaving base open. Pull the pattern piece off and trim close to stitching. Clip curves, especially between the two spikes of the crest. Turn crest right side out, turn

under and baste raw edges **(fig. 2)**, and stuff. Pin the crest to the wading bird's head with appliqué pins and handstitch to bird with ladder stitch or your preferred handstitch **(fig. 3)**.

20 Draw eyes with disappearing ink fabric marker. Embroider eyes with two strands of brown embroidery floss using satin stitch for eyeballs and stem stitch for eyebrows.

flamingo

The plastic pink flamingo is an iconic lawn ornament; I thought it would be fun to make a refined fabric flamingo to display indoors. The challenge was to make a bird with a neck that curved downward. I love the feeling of motion in this pose, as though the flamingo is about to dig its beak into the sand in search of some shrimp to eat. Use 16-gauge brass wire so that the legs will hold their shape and be patient as you balance this bird. I used a print fabric with a large repeat for the bird body and feathers, giving the impression of several colors of fabric together.

FINISHED SIZE
12" (30.5 cm) tall

MATERIALS
Print fabric for side body, head, head gusset, and feathers ½ yd (45.5 cm)

White or natural fabric for wing and tail bases and underbody, ⅛ yd (11.5 cm)

Yellow and black fabric scraps for beak, 6" × 3" (15 × 7.5 cm) of each

Wool stuffing, 12 oz (340 g)

16-gauge brass wire, 48" (122 cm)

Floral tape in a color to coordinate with print fabric

Brown embroidery floss

TOOLS
Basic birdmaking tool kit

Clear tape

PATTERN PIECES (page 153)
Side Body + Head (tape together, cut 1, cut 1 reverse)

Underbody (cut 1, cut 1 reverse)

Back Gusset (cut 1)

Head Gusset (cut 1)

Wing (cut 2, cut 2 reverse)

Tail (cut 2)

Beak (cut as directed)

Beak Gusset (cut 1)

NOTES
● Before you begin, read Basic Bird-making Techniques, pages 19–39, for detailed instructions on the birdmaking process.

● Add ¼" (6 mm) seam allowance to all pattern pieces except where noted.

1 Prewash and iron all fabrics. Trace pattern pieces onto freezer paper and cut out. Be sure to cut left and right versions of Side Body and Head, Underbody, Beak, and Wing. Attach Head to Side Body pattern with clear tape.

2 Iron freezer paper pattern pieces onto fabric, matte side up, and cut left and right Side Body pieces, left and right Underbody pieces, one Head Gusset, and one Back Gusset from print fabric (use a scrap of fabric as a press cloth when ironing over tape to prevent melting). Transfer all markings.

3 Sew an oval dart on each Underbody piece. Pin legs down to keep them out of the way while you do the next step.

4 Pin Underbody pieces, right sides together, along top edge. Stitch from point A to point B and from point C to point D, leaving a 1" (2.5 cm) opening in the center of the seam for turning.

5 Pin one Underbody to one Side Body, right sides together, with the sewn dart pointed upward. Stitch along the bottom of the bird, leaving an opening at the base of the leg for inserting wire. Repeat with other Underbody and Side Body so that the bottom of the flamingo is now sewn.

6 Pin Head Gusset to top of head on one Side Body, right sides together. Sew from point E to point F. Pin other side of Head Gusset to other Side Body and sew from point E to point F.

flamingo
legs + feet

7 Pin Back Gusset to the back of one Side Body, right sides together. Sew from point H to point J **(fig. 1)**. Pin other side of Back Gusset to other Side Body and sew from point H to point J.

8 Sew remaining body seams (from point A to point F and then from point E to point H and from point J to point D) so that now the flamingo's body is sewn completely, with an opening for turning and stuffing in the underbody seam and openings at the base of each leg for inserting the wire.

9 Clip all curves, especially near the legs. Reinforce seams with additional stitching as needed. Use forceps to gently pull the legs into the body, then the tail, and finally the head. Gently turn the flamingo right side out through the opening left in the underbody seam, pulling the head through the opening first. Use forceps to push the legs and tail out. Stuff the flamingo with small pieces of stuffing, beginning at the head and working your way down, packing the stuffing very firmly as you go. Pay particular attention to the long neck, being sure to stuff very firmly so that it is smooth.

10 When you have about ½" (1.3 cm) of the bird body remaining to be stuffed, pause to insert the 16-gauge wire.

11 Finish stuffing, pushing small bits of stuffing into the body to cover the wire and hold it in place. Push stuffing bit by bit into the leg openings and the tail. Push as much stuffing into the flamingo as possible.

12 Bend the wire to make the feet. The total length of the finished leg should be about 8" (20.5 cm). The total length of the longest toe should be about 2" (5 cm). Balance the bird so it stands on its own.

13 Push a bit more stuffing into the body and close the opening with ladder stitch. About 3" (7.5 cm) down the leg, create a bend in the wire to give the flamingo a natural stance. Rebalance the bird.

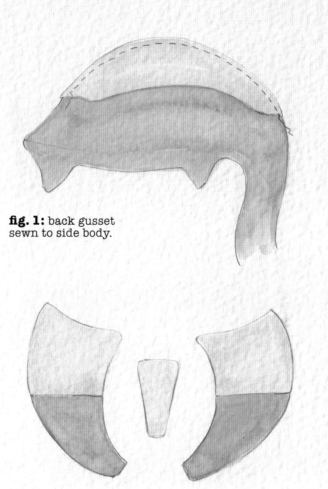

fig. 1: back gusset sewn to side body.

fig. 2: left + right beak sections cut from pieced fabric, and beak gusset.

flamingo
wings +
tail

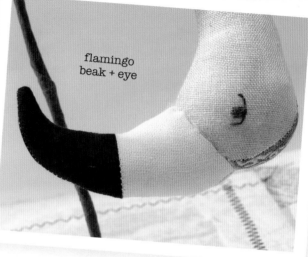

flamingo
beak + eye

14 Wrap the legs and feet with floral tape. Two or three layers of tape may be necessary to give the legs some heft. At the bend, wrap the floral tape more than on the rest of the leg to create some thickness and make the bend appear as a joint.

15 Using the Wing and Tail pattern pieces, create the bases for two wings and one tail and cover the wings and tail with looped feathers made from torn strips of fabric.

16 Pin tail to stuffed flamingo body and tack down with a few handstitches. Pin wings to flamingo body and tack down.

17 Stitch a 6" × 3" (15 × 7.5 cm) scrap of yellow quilting cotton to a 6" × 3" (15 × 7.5 cm) scrap of black quilting cotton, right sides together, along the 6" (15 cm) edge. Press seam toward black fabric and trim seam allowance to ⅛" (3 mm). Fold pieced fabric in half perpendicular to the seam, with right sides together. Iron the Beak pattern piece to the wrong side of this pieced fabric, aligning the dotted line on the pattern piece with the seam on the fabric. Cut out Beak, leaving a ¼" (6 mm) seam allowance. Pull off pattern piece. Flip remaining fabric over and repeat, so you have two mirror-image beak sections cut from pieced fabric. Iron the Beak Gusset pattern piece to a scrap of yellow quilting cotton. Cut out, leaving a ¼" (6 mm) seam allowance. Pull off pattern piece **(fig. 2, page 107)**.

18 Using appliqué pins, pin the Beak Gusset to one Beak piece, right sides together, and sew from point G1 to point H1. Pin the Beak Gusset to the other Beak piece and sew from point G2 to point H2. Sew around the rest of the beak, leaving the base open for turning and stuffing. Trim seam allowance to ⅛" (3 mm).

19 Clip curves on the beak and turn it right side out, using forceps. Fold the raw edge inward and baste in place. Stuff the beak firmly. Pin it to the flamingo's face and stitch it in place using small ladder stitches or your preferred handstitch.

20 Draw the eyes with a disappearing ink fabric marker. Using two strands of brown embroidery floss, stitch eyebrows using a stem stitch and stitch eyeballs using a satin stitch (see page 137).

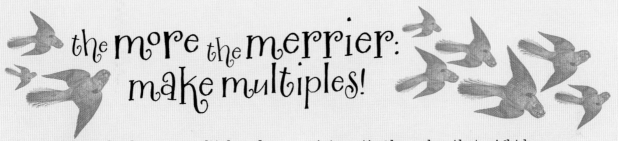

the more the merrier: make multiples!

For a striking display, sew multiples of a single type of bird. You can use the same fabrics for all, so the birds are nearly identical, or use similar but different fabrics so that there are variations in each bird. Group an odd number of birds for the most effective display, as in the photograph of wrens on page 46. Pose them so that they are looking at one another as though in conversation to evoke an appealing narrative.

Consider creative ways to display the birds together. Go on a nature walk to collect interesting branches that might become perches, purchase a wooden birdhouse at the craft store to paint and embellish, or shop an estate sale to find interesting objects for a tableau that complements your birds. A few simple brackets from the hardware store can transform an interesting piece of weathered wood into a wall-mounted shelf for a bird to stand on. An old birdcage with a little fabric bird perched inside is magical. These are just a few ideas to get you started; you'll no doubt discover your own.

gull

When I set out to design this gull, I wanted to make a bird with wings spread in flight. A heavyweight double-sided fusible interfacing—almost as stiff as cardboard—is the key to successfully building wings in flight. This heavyweight interfacing, available at fabric stores, can take a bit of brawn to work with, but it really allows you to create the look of wings in motion. Strung from the ceiling with legs pushed flush to the body and wings spread wide, this fabric gull is truly soaring.

FINISHED SIZE

11" (28 cm) wingspan, 9½" (24 cm) from beak to tail

MATERIALS

White fabric for body, wings, tail, and feathers, ½ yd (45.5 cm)

Scrap of brown fabric for beak

Heavyweight fusible interfacing

Wool stuffing, 10 oz (283.5 g)

16-gauge brass wire, 36" (91.5 cm)

Dark brown floral tape

White upholstery-weight thread

Brown embroidery floss

Fishing wire for hanging

TOOLS

Basic birdmaking tool kit

PATTERN PIECES (page 154)

Side Body (cut 1, cut 1 reverse)

Underbody (cut 1, cut 1 reverse)

Head Gusset (cut 1)

Tail (from fabric, cut 2; from interfacing, cut 1)

Wing (from fabric, cut 2, cut 2 reverse; from interfacing, cut 2)

Beak (cut as directed)

NOTES

- Before you begin, read Basic Birdmaking Techniques, pages 19–39, for detailed instructions on the birdmaking process.

- Add ¼" (6 mm) seam allowance to all pattern pieces except where noted.

1 Prewash and iron all fabrics. Trace all pattern pieces onto freezer paper and cut out. Be sure to cut left and right versions of Side Body, Underbody, and Wing.

2 Iron freezer paper pattern pieces onto fabric, matte side up, and cut left and right Side Body pieces, left and right Underbody pieces, and one Head Gusset from bird body fabric. Transfer all markings.

3 Pin Underbody pieces, right sides together, along top edge. Stitch, using a ¼" (6 mm) seam, from point A to point B and from point C to point D, leaving a 1" (2.5 cm) opening in the center of the seam for turning and stuffing.

4 Pin one Underbody to one Side Body, right sides together. Stitch along the bottom of the bird, leaving the base of the leg open for inserting wire. Pin the other edge of that same Underbody to the Side Body and stitch. Repeat with the other Underbody and Side Body so that the bottom of the gull is now sewn.

5 Pin Head Gusset to top of head on one Side Body, right sides together. Sew from point E to point F. Pin other side of Head Gusset to other Side Body and sew from point E to point F.

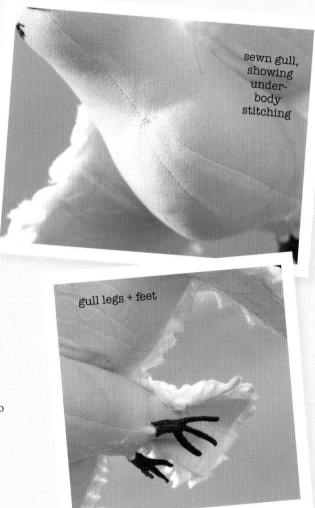

sewn gull, showing under-body stitching

gull legs + feet

gull tail

7 Clip all curves, especially near the legs. Reinforce seams as needed. Use forceps to gently pull the legs into the body, then the tail, and finally the head. Gently turn the gull right side out through the opening left in the underbody seam, pulling the head through the opening first. Use forceps to push the legs and tail out. Stuff the gull with small pieces of stuffing, beginning at the head and working your way down, packing the stuffing very firmly as you go.

8 When about ½" (1.3 cm) of the gull remains unstuffed, pause to insert the 16-gauge wire.

9 Finish stuffing, pushing small bits of stuffing into the body to cover the wire and hold it in place. Push stuffing bit by bit into the leg openings and the tail. Push as much stuffing into the gull as possible.

10 Form the feet. The length of the finished leg should be about 1" (2.5 cm). The length of the longest toe should be about 1½" (3.8 cm). Don't worry about balancing this bird; the legs and feet are made flush with the body in the next step.

11 Close the opening with ladder stitch. Wrap the legs and feet with floral tape. Bend the feet back toward the tail and push the legs back toward the tail to look like those of a bird in flight.

6 Sew remaining body seams (from point A to point F and then from point E to point D) so that now the gull's body is sewn completely, with an opening for turning and stuffing on the underbody seam and the bases of the legs open for inserting wire.

113

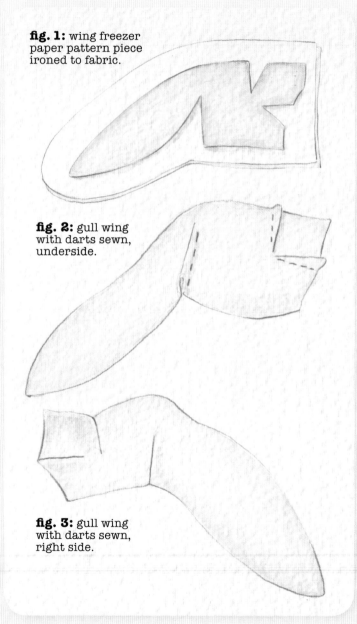

fig. 1: wing freezer paper pattern piece ironed to fabric.

fig. 2: gull wing with darts sewn, underside.

fig. 3: gull wing with darts sewn, right side.

gull wings + tail, shown from below

12 To make the wings, cut two pieces of white fabric and one piece of heavyweight interfacing, each about ½" (1.3 cm) larger than the Wing pattern in all dimensions. Sandwich the interfacing between the fabric layers and iron to fuse the interfacing to the top and bottom fabric layers. Iron a freezer paper Wing pattern piece on top **(fig. 1)**. To shape the wing, make and stitch the three darts indicated **(fig. 2)**. Trim excess fabric from stitched darts. Finish stitching around the Wing pattern piece. Pull pattern piece off and trim ⅛" (3 mm) from stitching line **(fig. 3)**. Repeat for other wing (remember that you are making a left and right wing that are mirror images of each other).

13 For tail, cut two pieces of white fabric and one piece of interfacing about ½" (1.3 cm) larger than the Tail pattern. Sandwich the interfacing between the fabric layers and iron the Tail pattern piece on top. Stitch around the pattern piece. Pull pattern piece off and trim ⅛" (3 mm) from stitching line.

14 Cover wings and tail in looped feathers made from strips of the same white fabric.

gull eye
+ beak

15 Pin tail to bird, curving it around the sides of the bird's body. Pin and tack down, using a heavy needle and upholstery-weight thread.

16 Shape wings by pushing the two darts at the tops of the wings downward to make the wings look as though they are spread in flight. Pin wings to gull's back and tack down just along the gull's back.

17 Iron the Beak pattern piece to a double layer of brown fabric, right sides together. Stitch around the edge of the freezer paper pattern piece, leaving base open. Trim close to stitching. Pull pattern piece off. Turn beak right side out, turn raw edge under and baste, stuff beak, and attach to bird with ladder stitch or your preferred handstitch.

18 Draw eyes with disappearing ink fabric marker. With two strands of brown embroidery floss, embroider eyeballs in satin stitch and eyebrows in stem stitch (see page 137).

19 Thread a needle with a single strand of fishing wire. Take one stitch through top of gull's back. Tie ends. Hang gull from the ceiling using a hook or nail.

hen & egg

For a few weeks one summer, we took care of two hens from a local farm. They lived in a coop in our yard, clucking and preening and resting right next to one another in the sunshine. Our daughters woke up early every morning to open the coop, letting the hens out to eat leftover food from our breakfast table. We were smitten. I created this hen and her eggs in tribute to our backyard chickens. Red is my favorite color, and I especially loved choosing a variety of deep reds for the wings and tail of this bird. She has a perky tail, made with a bit of heavyweight interfacing, and a stuffed wattle and comb. A clutch of eggs helps set the scene.

FINISHED SIZE

Hen, 11¼" (28.5 cm) tall;
eggs, 1½" (3.8 cm) in diameter

MATERIALS

White or natural fabric for side body, underbody, head gusset, wing bases, and tail base, ½ yd (45.5 cm)

3 or 4 different fabrics in red shades for feathers, crest, and wattle, ⅛ yd (11.5 cm) of each

Fabric scraps in light brown shades for beak and legs

White or natural fabric for eggs, ⅛ yd (11.5 cm)

Wool stuffing, 12 oz (340 g)

16-gauge brass wire, 36" (91.5 cm)

Brown floral tape

Heavyweight double-sided fusible interfacing, ¼ yd (23 cm)

Dark red or reddish-brown acrylic paint

White upholstery-weight thread

Dark brown embroidery floss

TOOLS

Basic birdmaking tool kit
Paintbrush

PATTERN PIECES (page 155)

Side Body (cut 1, cut 1 reverse)

Underbody (cut 1, cut 1 reverse)

Head Gusset (cut 1)

Wing (cut 2, cut 2 reverse)

Wattle (cut as directed)

Tail (from fabric, cut 2; from interfacing, cut 1)

Comb (cut as directed)

Top Beak (cut as directed)

Bottom Beak (cut as directed)

Egg (cut 5 for each egg)

NOTES

- Before you begin, read Basic Birdmaking Techniques, pages 19–39, for detailed instructions on the birdmaking process.
- Add ¼" (6 mm) seam allowance to all pattern pieces except where noted.

1 Prewash and iron all fabrics. Trace pattern pieces onto freezer paper and cut out. Be sure to cut left and right versions of Side Body, Underbody, and Wing.

2 Iron freezer paper pattern pieces onto fabric, matte side up, and cut left and right Side Body pieces, left and right Underbody pieces, and one Head Gusset from bird body fabric. Transfer all markings.

3 Sew an oval dart on each Underbody piece. Fold legs downward and pin down to keep them out of the way while you stitch the next step.

4 Pin Underbody pieces, right sides together, along top edge. Stitch from point A to point B and from point C to point D, leaving a 1" (2.5 cm) opening in the center of the seam for turning and stuffing.

5 Pin one Underbody to one Side Body, right sides together, with the dart pointed upward. Stitch along bottom of bird, leaving an opening at the base of the leg for inserting wire. Repeat with other Underbody and Side Body so that the bottom of the hen is now sewn.

6 Pin Head Gusset to top of head on one Side Body, right sides together. Sew from point E to point F. Pin other side of Head Gusset to other Side Body and sew from point E to point F.

7 Sew remaining body seams (from point A to point E and then from point F to point D) so that now the hen's body is sewn completely, with an opening for turning and stuffing on the underbody seam and openings at the base of each leg for inserting the wire.

hen legs + feet

8 Clip all curves, especially near the legs. Reinforce seams with additional stitching as needed. Use forceps to gently pull the legs into the body, then the tail, and finally the head. Gently turn the hen right side out through the opening left in the underbody seam, pulling the head through the opening first. Use forceps to push the legs, tail, and head out. Stuff the hen with small pieces of stuffing, beginning at the head and working your way down, packing the stuffing very firmly as you go.

9 When you have about ½" (1.3 cm) remaining to stuff, pause to insert the 16-gauge wire.

10 Finish stuffing, pushing small bits of stuffing into the body to cover the wire and hold it in place. Push stuffing bit by bit into the leg openings and the tail. Push as much stuffing into the hen as possible.

11 Form the legs and feet. The length of each finished leg should be about 1½" (3.8 cm). The length of the longest toe should be about 1" (2.5 cm). Balance the bird so it stands on its own.

12 Push a bit more stuffing into the bird's body and close the opening with ladder stitch. Wrap the legs and feet with floral tape. Wrap the legs and feet with torn strips of fabric, leaving the talons exposed. Wrap legs and feet with thread (I used red).

13 For the tail, cut a piece of heavyweight inter-facing and two pieces of one of the red fabrics ½" (1.3 cm) larger than the Tail pattern piece. Place the two pieces of fabric, wrong sides together, with the interfacing sandwiched in between. Fuse the interfacing between the two pieces of fabric. Iron the Tail pattern piece on top of this sandwich. Stitch around the tail and cut it out ⅛" (3 mm) from the stitching line.

14 Paint the outer edges and side edges of the sewn tail with dark red acrylic paint so that it will not stand out once the red feathers are sewn down **(fig. 1)**. Let the paint dry completely.

15 Using the Wing pattern piece, make two wing bases. Cover the wings with looped feathers made from torn strips of the fabrics in red shades.

16 The tail on the hen has feathers on both sides because it rises up off the bird's body and can be seen from both the back and the front. To do this, sew a row of looped feathers on one side of the tail, beginning on the widest part. Flip tail over and sew an identical row on other side. Sew a second row of feathers overlapping the first. Flip and sew a second row on the other side. Continue to sew rows on both sides for five rows. The last few rows are sewn only on one side because the other side will be attached to the bird's body **(fig. 2)**.

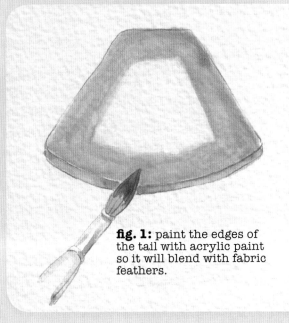

fig. 1: paint the edges of the tail with acrylic paint so it will blend with fabric feathers.

fig.2: hen tail has feathers on both sides; the last few rows are sewn on one side only.

17 Pin tail to stuffed hen body, curving it around the body so that it sticks up in the air. Pin down and then tack down using upholstery-weight thread and a heavy needle. Pin wings to hen body and tack down. Rebalance the bird.

18 Iron Top Beak freezer paper pattern piece to a double layer of fabric, right sides together. Stitch around edge of freezer paper, leaving base open. Pull pattern piece off and trim close to stitching and lower edge. Turn beak right side out, turn raw edge under and baste, stuff beak, and sew onto bird with handstitching. Repeat with Bottom Beak pattern.

19 Draw eyes onto head with disappearing fabric marker. Using two strands of brown embroidery floss, embroider eyeballs with satin stitch and eyebrows with stem stitch.

20 To make the comb, cut two matching scraps of fabric ¼" (6 mm) larger than the Comb pattern piece. Place fabric scraps with wrong sides together and iron Comb pattern piece on top. Stitch around comb, leaving bottom open for stuffing. Trim comb ⅛" (3 mm) from stitching and lower edge of pattern piece. Pull pattern piece off. Comb is not turned. Fold raw edges at bottom of comb inward and baste. Using forceps, stuff firmly with tiny bits of stuffing, paying particular attention to the small grooves and points on top of the comb. Attach comb to hen's head with ladder stitch.

full hen in profile

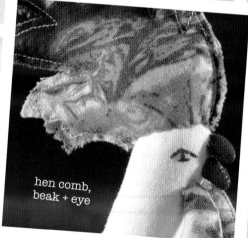

hen comb, beak + eye

hen tail from underneath

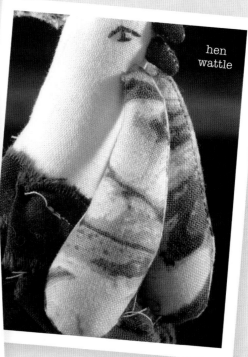

hen wattle

21 To make wattles, cut two matching scraps of fabric, each 5" × 5" (12.5 × 12.5 cm), and place them right sides together. Iron Wattle pattern piece on top. Stitch around pattern piece, leaving the top open for turning and stuffing. Cut wattle out, cutting ⅛" (3 mm) outside stitching lines. Carefully reach forceps into each wattle and pull right side out. Fold raw edge inward and baste. Stuff firmly. Repeat for second wattle. Pin and sew the wattles one at a time to hen with ladder stitch or your preferred handstitch.

22 To make the egg, cut five 3" × 4" (7.5 × 10 cm) scraps of white fabric. Iron Egg pattern piece to each scrap and cut out, adding a ⅛" (3 mm) seam allowance. Sew one piece to another, beginning at point G and ending at point H. Continue attaching wedges until you get to the fifth wedge. For the fifth wedge, leave a ½" (1.3 cm) opening halfway between point G and point H for turning and stuffing. Check all seams, especially at the top and bottom of the egg, and reinforce as necessary. Turn egg right side out using forceps. Fold raw edges of opening inward. Stuff firmly, rolling the egg in your hands to make it round. Close opening with ladder stitch. Make additional eggs as desired.

121

peacock

The peacock is the most regal of birds;
its extravagant tail and proud stance
make it a real showstopper.
Make the peacock in neutral tones for
an unusual and eye-catching bird
or use traditional peacock blues
and greens. The luxurious tail is an
opportunity to use interesting fabrics.
I used strips of vintage lace with torn
strips of quilting cotton, but you could
try strips of velvet or sparkly fabrics.
Although the peacock looks complex,
it's not more difficult to sew than
smaller birds, though the tail is
labor-intensive. Think of it as a blank
canvas to lavishly embellish!

FINISHED SIZE
13½" (34.5 cm) tall to
top of crest; 17" (43 cm)
from front of body to
end of tail

MATERIALS
Two different cotton fabrics for side body,
head gusset, wing bases, and tail base,
⅓ yd (30.5 cm) each

Four different fabrics for feathers,
¼ yd (23 cm) each

Wool stuffing, 16 oz (454 g)

18-gauge aluminum wire for
crest embellishment, 15" (38 cm)

16-gauge brass wire for legs
and feet, 36" (91.5 cm)

Dark brown floral tape

Brown, silver, and white embroidery floss

TOOLS
Basic birdmaking tool kit

Clear tape

OPTIONAL: Round craft punch for
crest, cutting mat or stack of old
newspapers, and hammer

PATTERN PIECES
(pages 156–157)

Side Body + Head (tape Head to Side
Body; cut 1, cut 1 reverse as directed)

Underbody (cut 1, cut 1 reverse)

Head Gusset (cut 1)

Beak (cut as directed)

Tail + Tail End (tape Tail to
Tail End; cut 2)

Wing (cut 2, cut 2 reverse)

NOTES
- Before you begin, read Basic Birdmaking Techniques, pages 19–39, for
  detailed instructions on the birdmaking
  process.
- Add ¼" (6 mm) seam allowance to all
  pattern pieces except where noted.

legs + feet wrapped with floral tape, fabric, + thread, with talons exposed

peacock tail

1 Prewash and iron all fabrics. Trace pattern pieces onto freezer paper and cut out.

2 Attach Side Body to Head pattern piece with clear tape. Attach Tail to Tail End pattern piece with clear tape. Be sure to trace left and right versions of the combined Side Body and Head.

3 Piece together ¼ yd (23 cm) of one color of body fabric with ½ yd (45.5 cm) of the other color of body fabric with a ¼" (6 mm) seam along one long edge. Press seam to one side. Using a scrap of fabric as a press cloth over tape to prevent tape from melting, iron taped Side Body + Head pattern piece, matte side up, onto the wrong side of pieced fabric, with tape line on pattern piece matched up to seam line of fabric. Cut out Side Body **(fig. 1)**. Iron pattern piece to right side of pieced-together fabric, matching up taped line to seam line again, and cut out **(fig. 2)**. You now have two mirror-image Side Body pieces. Transfer all markings.

4 Cut out Head Gusset from same fabric as top part of Side Body. Cut out left and right Underbody from body fabric. Transfer all markings.

5 Sew oval dart on each Underbody. Fold leg down and pin down to keep it out of the way while you stitch the next step.

6 Pin Underbody pieces, right sides together, along top edge. Stitch along the top edge from point A to point B and from point C to point D, leaving a 1" (2.5 cm) opening in the center of the seam for turning and stuffing.

7 Pin one Underbody to one Side Body, right sides together, with the dart pointed upward. Stitch along the bottom of the bird, leaving the base of the leg open for inserting the wire. Repeat with other Underbody and Side Body so that the bottom of the peacock is now sewn.

8 Pin Head Gusset to top of head on one Side Body, right sides together. Sew from point E to point F. Pin other side of Head Gusset to other Side Body and sew from point E to point F.

9 Sew remaining body seams so that now the peacock's body is sewn completely, with an opening for turning and stuffing on the underbody seam and the base of the legs open for wire insertion.

10 Reinforce any weak seams. Clip all curves, especially near the legs. Use forceps to gently pull the legs into the body, then the tail and finally the head. Gently turn the peacock right side out through the opening left in the underbody seam, pulling the head through the opening first. Use forceps to push the legs and tail out.

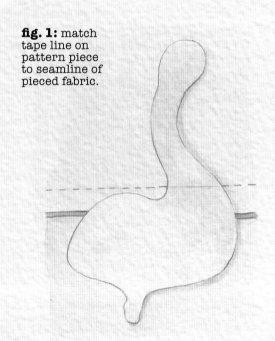

fig. 1: match tape line on pattern piece to seamline of pieced fabric.

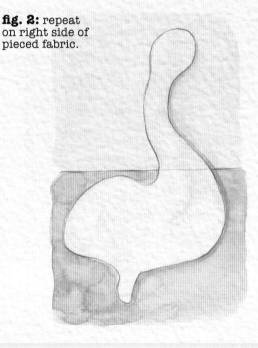

fig. 2: repeat on right side of pieced fabric.

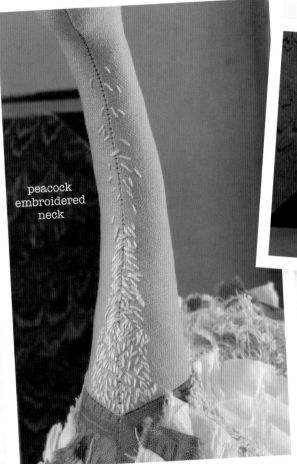

peacock
embroidered
neck

peacock
chest

peacock
crest, beak
+ eyes

11 Stuff the peacock with small pieces of stuffing, beginning at the head and working your way down, packing the stuffing very firmly as you go. Pay particular attention to stuffing the neck being sure that it is firm and not lumpy.

12 When you have about ¼" (6 mm) from the bottom of the peacock remaining to be stuffed, pause to insert the 16-gauge wire.

13 Finish stuffing, pushing small bits of stuffing into the body to cover the wire and hold it in place. Push stuffing bit by bit into the leg openings and the tail. Push as much stuffing into the peacock as possible.

14 Form the feet. The total length of the finished leg should be about 1" (2.5 cm). The total length of the longest toe should be about 1½" (3.8 cm). Be sure not to make the legs too long because this is a relatively heavy bird, and longer legs will make it difficult to balance and maintain stability.

15 Push a bit more stuffing into the bird's body and close the opening with ladder stitch. Wrap the legs and feet with floral tape. Wrap again with torn strips of fabric and then again with thread. Leave the toenails exposed.

16 Sew two wing bases and a tail base, using Wing pattern piece and taped Tail pattern piece. Create looped feathers for the wings and tail, alternating colors as you go to create a pleasing look. Lace fabric makes pretty loops for this elegant bird. Pin tail to peacock body and tack down with ladder stitch or your preferred handstitch. Pin wings to peacock body and tack down.

17 Iron Beak pattern piece, matte side up, to a double layer of fabric, right sides together. Sew directly around the freezer paper, leaving base of beak open. Trim close to stitching. Turn beak right side out, turn raw edge under and baste, stuff beak, and pin to bird. Stitch to head using ladder stitch or your preferred handstitch. With a single strand of silver embroidery floss, add a few decorative stitches to each side of the beak.

18 Draw eyes with disappearing ink fabric marker. With two strands of brown floss, embroider eyeballs using satin stitch and eyebrow using stem stitch. With two strands of white floss, embroider whites of eyes using satin stitch (see page 137).

19 Cut three lengths of 18-gauge aluminum wire, each 2½" (6.5 cm) long. Fold each length of wire in half. Poke wire through peacock's head so that fold in wire is buried inside head and ends of wire stick out. There will be six wire ends sticking out of peacock's head all together. Put a dab of craft glue at the base of each wire where it sticks out of peacock's head to hold it in place. Let glue dry.

20 Cut 12 small circles from colorful cotton fabric or punch circles from fabric using a craft punch on a stack of old newspapers. Apply dabs of glue to two circles. Sandwich the tip of one length of wire between the two circles and press to adhere. Repeat for all six lengths of wire to create crest.

21 Using two strands of white embroidery floss, use straight stitch to create feathery detail along the bird's neck, as shown.

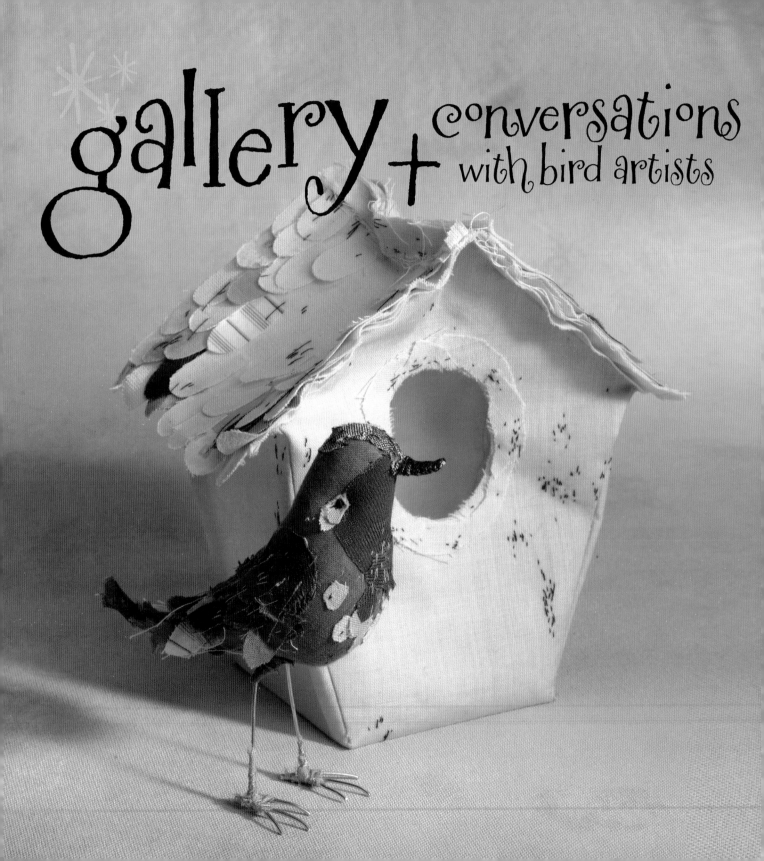

gallery + conversations with bird artists

ABIGAIL BROWN

Abigail Brown earned a degree in illustration and textiles in 2003. She lives in London amid mountains of fabric scraps and loose threads. Her greatest passion is working with fabric, a familiar medium since her early years spent with her seamstress grandmother. See more of her work at abigail-brown.co.uk.

Q. How did you begin sewing birds?

A. *I'd been drawing birds for a while, making them out of clay and just developing an interest in them generally. A friend had a decorative birdcage and asked me if I would make her a fabric bird to sit in it, so I did. I started a whole flock of them to exhibit and it just went from there.*

Q. You make the legs of your birds with exposed wire that is wrapped with thread and fabric scraps just around the toes. Do you have tips for balancing birds?

A. *It's a series of small adjustments. You stand the bird on a surface, hold firmly with one hand down on the feet, and then with the other hand, slowly move the bird back and forth a little to find the balance spot . . . it can take a while, but moving them is really the best way.*

Q. What kinds of fabrics do you use for your birds? Where do you find fabric?

A. *I've always collected fabric scraps, since my early years with my grandmother, who was a seamstress. She collected her scraps in what she termed a "raggy bag" and I continue this practice. I collect scraps from other projects, I recycle old clothing, and I buy new fabrics in fabric shops wherever I might be. I'm always collecting, even if I never quite know what a piece will be used for, or when.*

Q. Your birds have a deconstructed look, with raw edges and handstitches to evoke wing and tail feathers. How do you achieve this effect?

A. *I work with all the varied colors, tones, patterns, and textures in the scraps of fabric that I collect, and use them to create layers, which I then sew and embellish.*

Q. What is it about birds that you are specifically drawn to?

A. *I love their size and the detail in them; I like to watch their jerky, bobbing movements and the quizzical twists of their heads, how they dance along on the ground and how gracefully they swoop through the skies. They are just a delight to watch!*

Q. For the birds you've made that are in nests or on branches, how do you make the nests, and how do you affix the birds to branches?

A. *The nests are woven scraps of fabric, securely sewn with intermittent stitches to keep them together. The birds on branches have wire from their feet fed through holes drilled in the branch and secured.*

Opposite and below: Found fabrics and loose threads make Abigail's birds quirky and charming.

ANN WOOD

Ann Wood is an artist in Brooklyn, New York, where she lives near beautiful Prospect Park. She makes things, paints, and draws for her life and livelihood. Ann works with mostly found and salvaged materials, with a focus on transformation: cardboard boxes from the grocery store become turreted castles and follies and windmills, and wretched and ruined old petticoats and gowns become roiling boiling seas for papier-mâché ships and boats. See more of her work at annwoodhandmade.com.

Q: How did you begin sewing birds?

A: *In 2005, I was designing a holiday window for a shop on Orchard Street on the Lower East Side of Manhattan, and I had recently acquired a few ruined antique gowns and bits of gowns—really ruined—incredibly fragile and beautiful with exquisite details and lace. I was fascinated by them and wanted to incorporate them into the window. The colors and frayed feathery textures inspired birds.*

Q: Where do you find inspiration for your sewing projects?

A: *I like to work with vintage and antique garments. There is a kind of affection and tenderness in the reuse and repurposing of things that were once personal and perhaps treasured possessions. Much of my inspiration comes from these materials.*

Q: Tell me about the process of transforming a dress into a bird.

A: *A large part of the fun for me is looking for the garments and scraps I work with. I haunt eBay looking for things, visit flea markets almost every weekend, and attend antique clothing shows. Sometimes, the limitations presented by the condition of a disintegrating garment become the source of inspiration. An Edwardian lawn gown—discolored, tissue-thin, and unsewable—becomes feathers for a willet in winter plumage.*

Q: Your owls have wonderful names and expressive faces. Why do owls appeal to you?

A: *I love naming the owls. Many of my owls are inspired by fictional characters; for example, Michael Henchard, the Mayor of Casterbridge, is one of my favorite characters in all of English literature. Lately I've been making scoundrels—Iago and Chillingworth, the most scoundrelly of all the scoundrels. He surprised me. He is made from a moth-eaten, tattered antique mourning bodice.*

Q: You also design shop windows. How do you set a scene for your birds?

A: *My windows usually reflect the ideas I've been fascinated with my whole life: smallness, intricacies, miniaturization, collections, repetition; lost or abandoned things discovered and rescued; the idea of haunted and enchanted places, things, and creatures. I like to use unassuming materials, cardboard, paper, and other discarded things. I love the idea of giving the humblest and most common materials, the tired, dispirited, and faded things, new importance and meaning.*

Opposite and above: Ann gives new life to vintage and distressed garments in her beautifully detailed birds.

131

TAMAR MOGENDORFF

Born and raised in Israel, artist Tamar Mogendorff now lives in New York, where she makes fabric animals in her own distinctive unconstructed style. The beauty of Tamar's work lies in the rough stitching and unfinished edges that lend each piece a truly handmade sensibility. Tamar uses new and vintage fabrics to sew three-dimensional fabric objects imbued with personality. See more of Tamar's work at tmogy.com.

Q. How did you begin making soft sculpture?

A. *I'd been sewing dolls and objects from fabric as a hobby. People wanted to buy them and I started putting more time into it. One day I decided to quit my job and just focus on sewing. I didn't plan it. Still, everything I make begins with something I make for myself.*

Q. What inspired you to make birds?

A. *Sewing birds began with an idea I had to make a fabric birdcage. I was drawn in by the idea of making a whole habitat. I like how the cage interferes with space. A caged bird gives you the feeling of a precious thing hanging in your space. You can almost hear the music of the bird inside. The cage makes the bird inside seem precious.*

Q. Tell me about your design process.

A. *I want the object to feel personal. For many years I sewed only by hand. To me, the whole feeling and personality comes through in the stitching. I like messy stitching. I am a very fast hand sewer, but my stitches are not even, and that is what people like about my work. It is more interesting, more personal, and less like something manufactured. In the end, the* fabric object is like an illustration, and each one has its own handwriting.

I do some sewing on my machine, but then I go over it by hand. I don't want to hide the stitches. I like to be able to control whether the stitches are close and intense or far apart. That's what gives it life, the story, the personal feeling, that someone was actually making it. You can feel the process behind it. At the same time, I want it to look effortless. Even though the stitches are visible, I want it to look well constructed and done with a light touch. I don't think too much; I just do. I can't do it otherwise.

Q. Tell me about a bird that you are most proud of.

A. *One of my most special birds is a swan that hangs on the wall. It is a play on taxidermy. Of course, it was never alive, but it looks like now it is coming alive and is about to fly off the wall. Birds don't have that much personality in their faces sometimes, but in their body and the fact that they fly and in their voices—that is what draws me in.*

Opposite and below: Visible, uneven stitching and an organic feel characterize Tamar's sculptures.

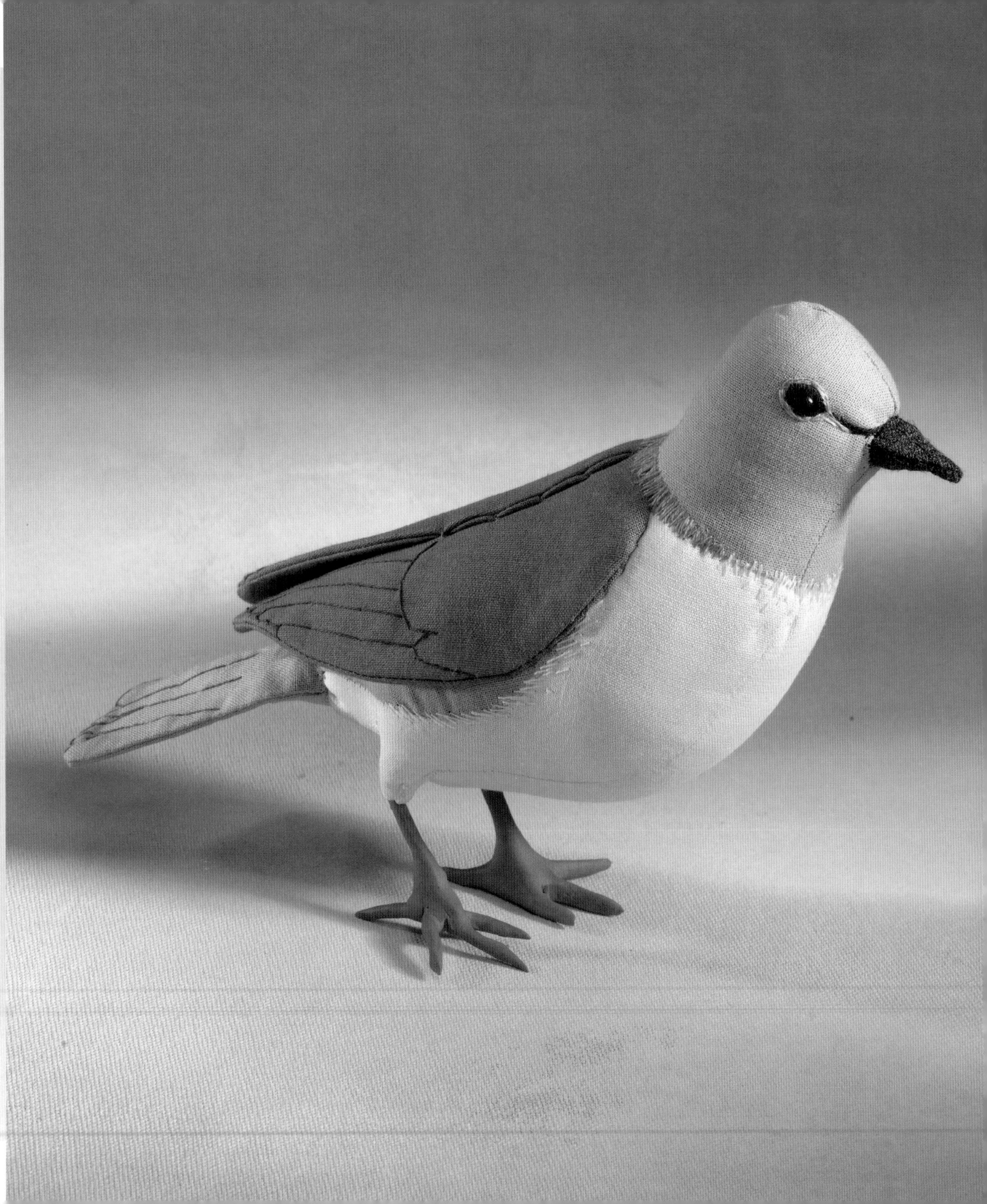

JENNIFER MUSKOPF

Jennifer Muskopf is an artist based in San Francisco. She makes soft sculptures and paintings depicting the strangeness of ordinary objects around us through careful detailing and fantastical juxtapositions. In 1993, Jennifer began working with fabric to make three-dimensional versions of the animals that often reside in her paintings. See more of Jennifer's work at jennifermuskopf.com.

Q: How did you begin sewing soft sculpture?

A: *After finishing art school, I was hired by the Vermont Studio Center as a staff artist. While there, I inherited my grandmother's old Kenmore sewing machine. I'd been using animal imagery in my paintings for many years, but had an interest in introducing pattern and color, so I used the sewing machine to construct animal parts and then stitched them together.*

Q: How do you make and insert the legs and feet on your birds?

A: *I tried using felt and gel medium and wire wrapped in yarn, but finally went with polymer clay. After the feet are baked and cooled, I slip them into the fabric leg holes of the bird's body, and stitch around them to make them stay in place.*

Q: What do you use for eyes?

A: *I hand-embroider all the eyes, faces, feathers, spots, and details.*

Q: What do you use to stuff your birds?

A: *I use polyester filling that is rough, not silky, so I can pack it firmly.*

Q: Do you have any tips for balancing birds?

A: *I did make a pelican with fabric feet that I filled with batting and quilted to make them stiff enough to stand on—but with that big bill, he still didn't balance. I added dressmaker weights to his tail for counterweight.*

Q: What kind of fabric do you use for your birds?

A: *My birds are made from wool, satin, and cotton fabrics. I like to use material that keeps its shape and can handle embroidery and being stressed with stuffing. I choose by color, texture, and thickness; I can't use fabrics that are too thick because they are too hard to turn.*

Q: Do you have a favorite tool?

A: *I have two favorite tools. The first is a modified chopstick. I cut the tip at an angle to make it rough enough to grab and push the filling in small amounts. The other is an awl with a wooden handle that I use to turn small parts.*

Q: What is it about birds that you are specifically drawn to?

A: *I was initially reluctant to make birds because of the intricate features and tiny parts; however, I felt compelled to create a series of common American birds together with large exotic cats but have them be the same scale. I really enjoyed the complexity of creating the bird parts and joining them into one creature. For another series, I focused on tropical birds native to Panama and Argentina, with their amazing color and variety. I love the intensity of color and pattern on birds!*

Opposite and above: Jennifer hand-embroiders eyes and uses polymer clay for legs and feet on her vivid bird sculptures.

RESOURCES

These sources for birdmaking tools and materials are current at press time.

FREEZER PAPER

Freezer paper is readily available at most grocery and discount stores. Precut 8½" × 11" (21.5 × 28 cm) printer-ready sheets of freezer paper are available at DollmakersJourney.com.

WOOL STUFFING

I purchase wool stuffing by the pound from West Earl Woolen Mills, an Amish mill. Ask for wool for stuffing dolls. At press time, cost was $6.40 per pound (454 g) plus shipping.

West Earl Woolen Mills
110 Cocalico Creek Rd.
Ephrata, PA 17522
(717) 859-2241

FLORAL TAPE

Floral tape in brown and white is available at most craft stores in the floral department. Florists may also be a source and sometimes have unusual colors, including black.

WIRE

Wire in 16-gauge and 18-gauge sizes is available at most hardware stores or online at Lowes.com.

FORCEPS AND TWEEZERS

Surgical forceps, also called hemostats, and long tweezers are available through dollmaking suppliers such as ClothDollSupply.com and DollmakersJourney.com. Forceps may also be available through your local hospital.

SIZZIX TOOLS FOR PUNCHED FEATHERS

I use Sizzix paddle punches, such as the leaf and hand paddle punches, to make punched feathers. These devices are no longer being made, but Sizzix operates an outlet store through eBay that sells this product. A die-cut machine, such as the Sizzix BIGkick Machine, can also be used for creating punched feathers.

Sizzix eBay Outlet Store   **Sizzix**
Stores.ebay.com/Sizzix-Outlet   *Sizzix.com*

FURTHER READING

For a comprehensive guide to birds, David Allen Sibley's Sibley Guide to Birds *(Knopf, 2000) can't be beat. For each bird that I make, I refer to this book to check on the shapes of beaks, wings, tails, and feet, and to get ideas for color combinations. I have found the following books to be instructive on soft-toy design. They are out of print but may be found through used booksellers.*

> *The Techniques of Soft Toymaking*, Enid Anderson (Batsford Publishing, 1982).

> *Good Design in Soft Toys*, Rudi De Sarigny (Taplinger Publishing, 1971).

I have also learned about fabric sculpture from the following books:

> *Anatomy of a Doll*, Susanna Oroyan (C&T Publishing, 1997).

> *Designing the Doll*, Susanna Oroyan (C&T Publishing, 1999).

I am inspired by Joseph Cornell's shadow-box assem-blages and recommend:

> *Joseph Cornell: Shadowplay . . . Eterniday* by Lynda Roscoe Hartigan, et al. (Thames & Hudson, 2003).

HANDSEWING STITCHES

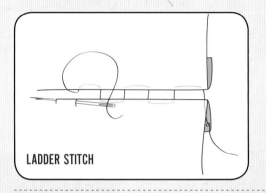

LADDER STITCH

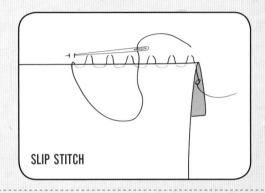

SLIP STITCH

EMBROIDERY STITCHES

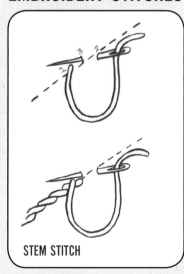

STEM STITCH

Stem stitch is used to create a graceful line. Working from left to right, bring the needle up at 1 and insert the needle ⅛" to ¼" (3 to 6 mm) away at 2. Bring the needle up halfway between 1 and 2, at 3. Keeping the newly created loop below the needle and stitch-line, pull the stitch taut. Continue by inserting the needle ⅛" to ¼" (3 to 6 mm) to the right of 2, then bring up the needle to the right of 2.

SATIN STITCH

Generally worked from left to right, satin stitch is most often used to fill in a shape or create a thick scallop-like edge. Bring the needle up at 1, insert at 2, and bring back up at 3. Repeat, keeping stitches close together to completely fill the space.

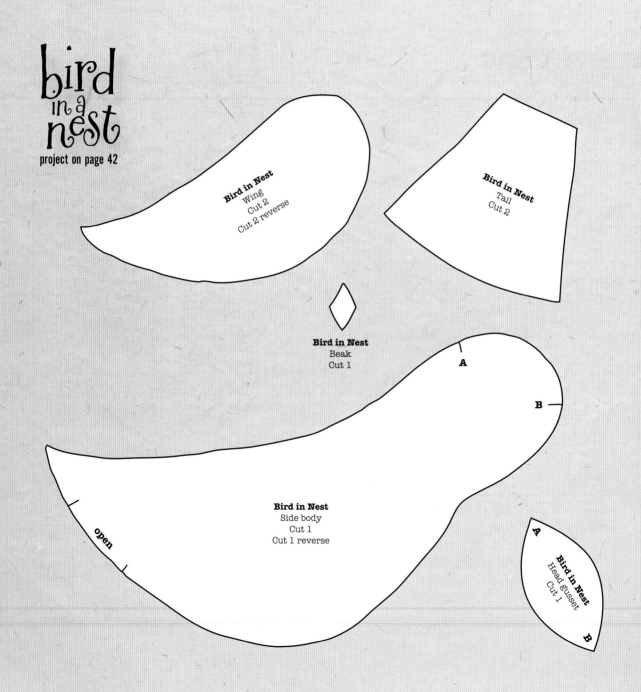

bird
in a
nest
project on page 42

Bird in Nest
Wing
Cut 2
Cut 2 reverse

Bird in Nest
Tail
Cut 2

Bird in Nest
Beak
Cut 1

A

B

Bird in Nest
Side body
Cut 1
Cut 1 reverse

open

A

Bird in Nest
Head gusset
Cut 1

B

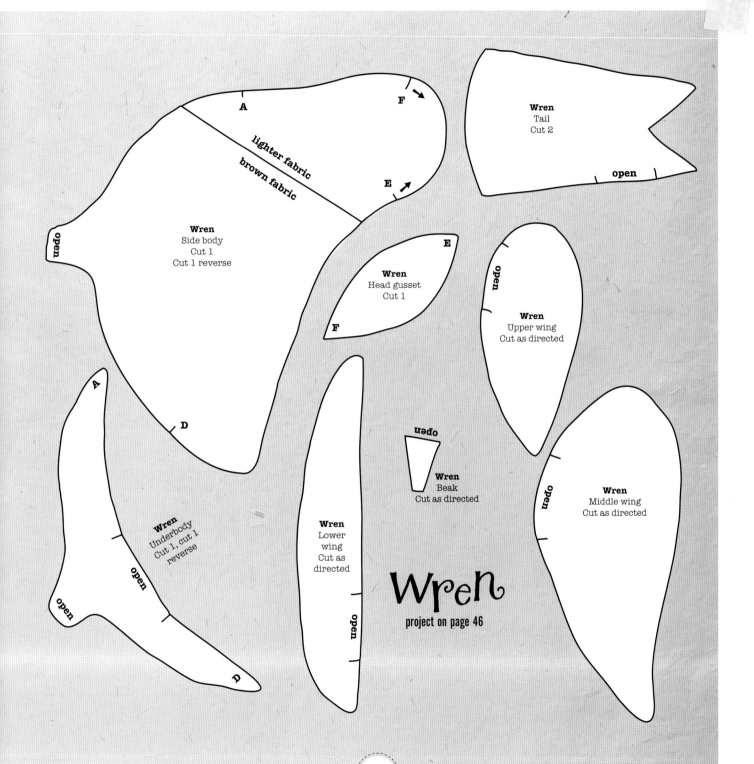

Wren
Tail
Cut 2

open

Wren
Side body
Cut 1
Cut 1 reverse

A

lighter fabric

brown fabric

F

E

open

Wren
Head gusset
Cut 1

E

F

Wren
Upper wing
Cut as directed

open

A

D

Wren
Underbody
Cut 1, cut 1
reverse

open

open

D

Wren
Lower
wing
Cut as
directed

open

open

Wren
Beak
Cut as directed

open

Wren
Middle wing
Cut as directed

Wren
project on page 46

Lark
Eye overlay
Cut as
directed

Lark
Side body
Cut 1
Cut 1 reverse

A

D

open

Lark
Tail
Cut 2

E

Lark
Head gusset
Cut 1

F

Lark
Eye mask
Cut as directed

Lark
Eye mask
Cut as directed

Lark
Wing
Cut 2
Cut 2 reverse

lark
project on page 50

A

B

C

D

dart

Lark
Underbody
Cut 1
Cut 1 reverse

open

Lark
Side head
Cut 2

E

F

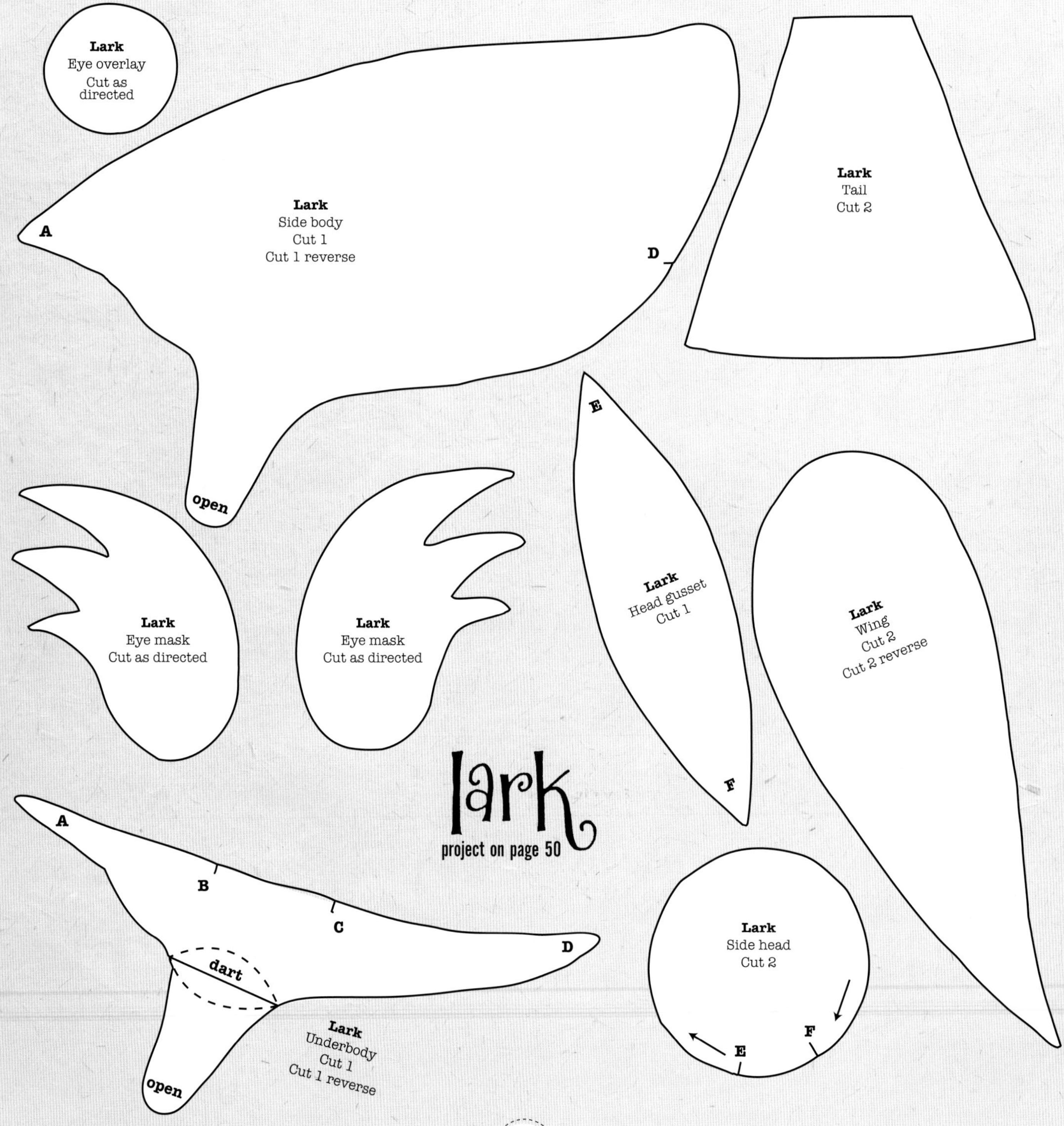

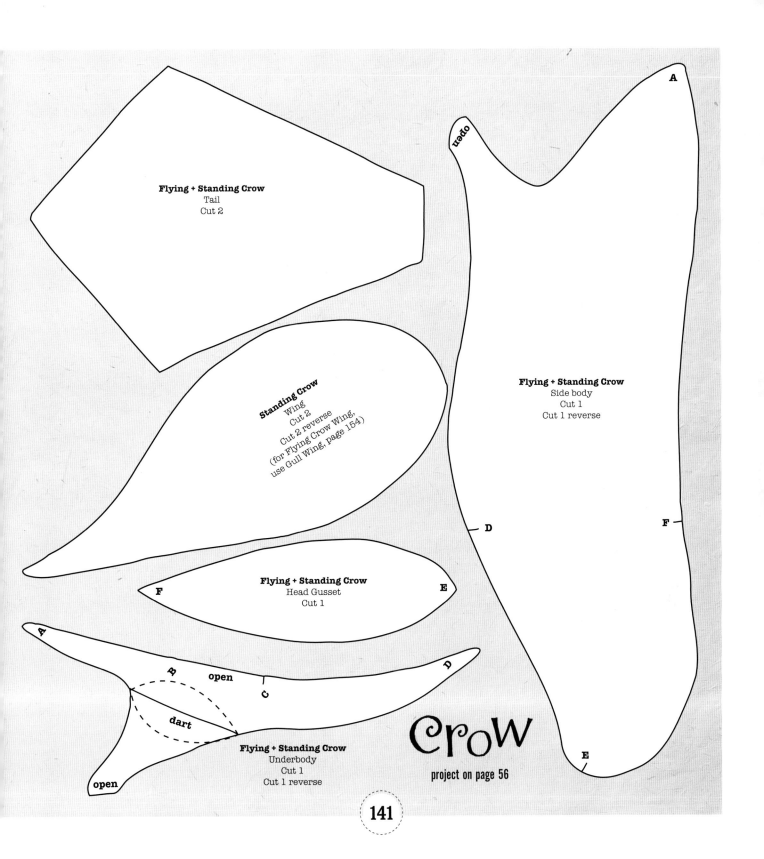

Flying + Standing Crow
Tail
Cut 2

Standing Crow
Wing
Cut 2
Cut 2 reverse
(for Flying Crow Wing,
use Gull Wing, page 154)

Flying + Standing Crow
Side body
Cut 1
Cut 1 reverse

open

A

D

F

E

Flying + Standing Crow
Head Gusset
Cut 1

F

E

A

B

open

C

D

dart

open

Flying + Standing Crow
Underbody
Cut 1
Cut 1 reverse

Crow

project on page 56

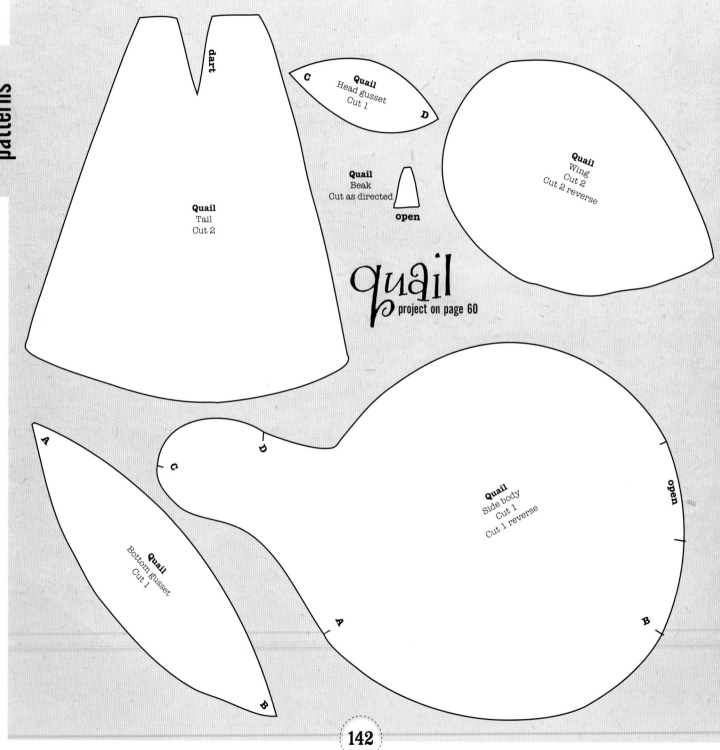

Quail
Tail
Cut 2

dart

C **Quail**
Head gusset
Cut 1 D

Quail
Beak
Cut as directed

open

Quail
Wing
Cut 2
Cut 2 reverse

quail
project on page 60

A

C

D

Quail
Bottom gusset
Cut 1

Quail
Side body
Cut 1
Cut 1 reverse

open

A

B

B

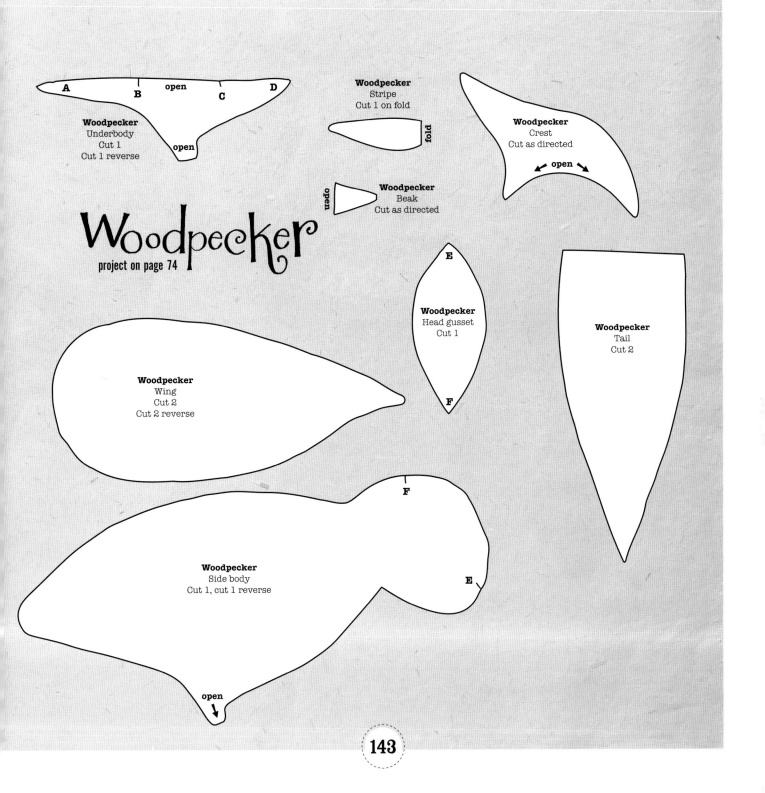

Woodpecker
Underbody
Cut 1
Cut 1 reverse

A   B   open   C   D

open

Woodpecker
Stripe
Cut 1 on fold

fold

Woodpecker
Crest
Cut as directed

open

open

Woodpecker
Beak
Cut as directed

Woodpecker

project on page 74

Woodpecker
Head gusset
Cut 1

E

F

Woodpecker
Tail
Cut 2

Woodpecker
Wing
Cut 2
Cut 2 reverse

Woodpecker
Side body
Cut 1, cut 1 reverse

F

E

open

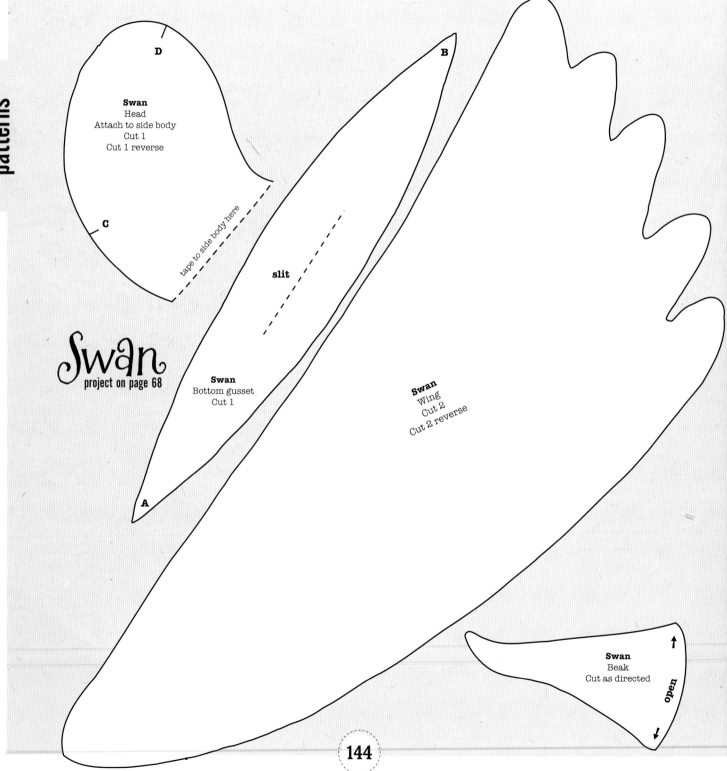

Swan
Head
Attach to side body
Cut 1
Cut 1 reverse

D

C

tape to side body here

Swan
project on page 68

slit

Swan
Bottom gusset
Cut 1

A

B

Swan
Wing
Cut 2
Cut 2 reverse

Swan
Beak
Cut as directed

open

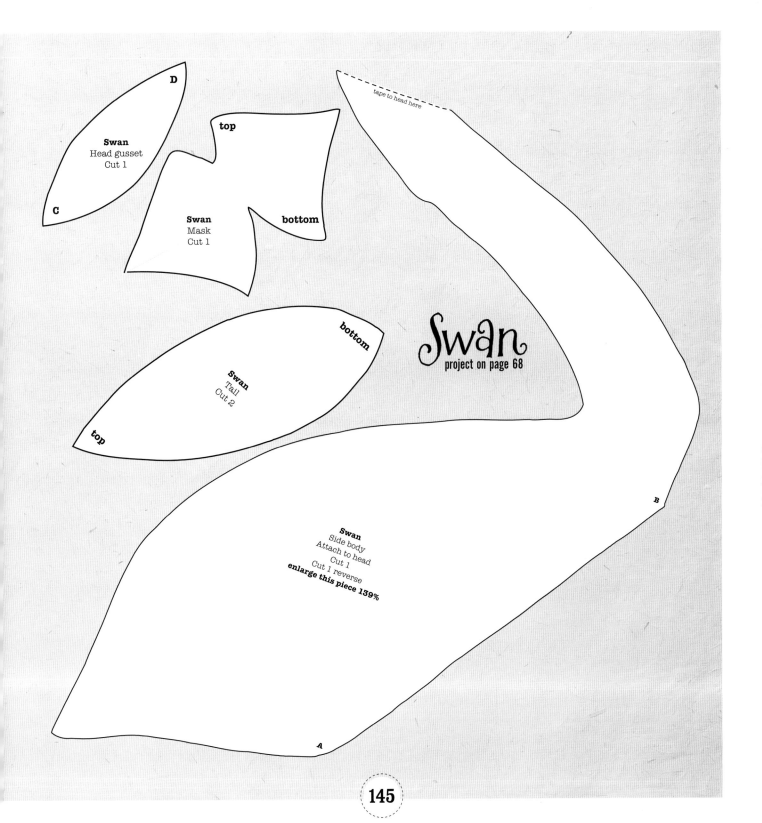

D

Swan
Head gusset
Cut 1

C

top

tape to head here

Swan
Mask
Cut 1

bottom

bottom

Swan
Tail
Cut 2

top

Swan
project on page 68

Swan
Side body
Attach to head
Cut 1
Cut 1 reverse
enlarge this piece 139%

B

A

145

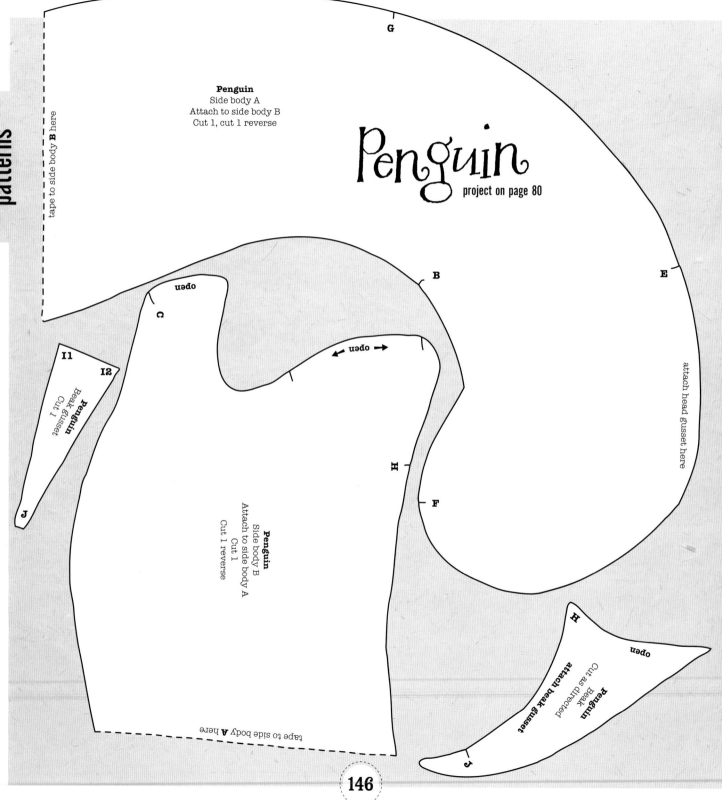

tape to side body **B** here

Penguin
Side body A
Attach to side body B
Cut 1, cut 1 reverse

Penguin
project on page 80

G

B

E

C

open

open

open

I1

I2

Penguin
Beak gusset
Cut 1

J

H

F

attach head gusset here

Penguin
Side body B
Attach to side body A
Cut 1
Cut 1 reverse

tape to side body **A** here

H

open

Penguin
Beak
Cut as directed

attach beak gusset

J

146

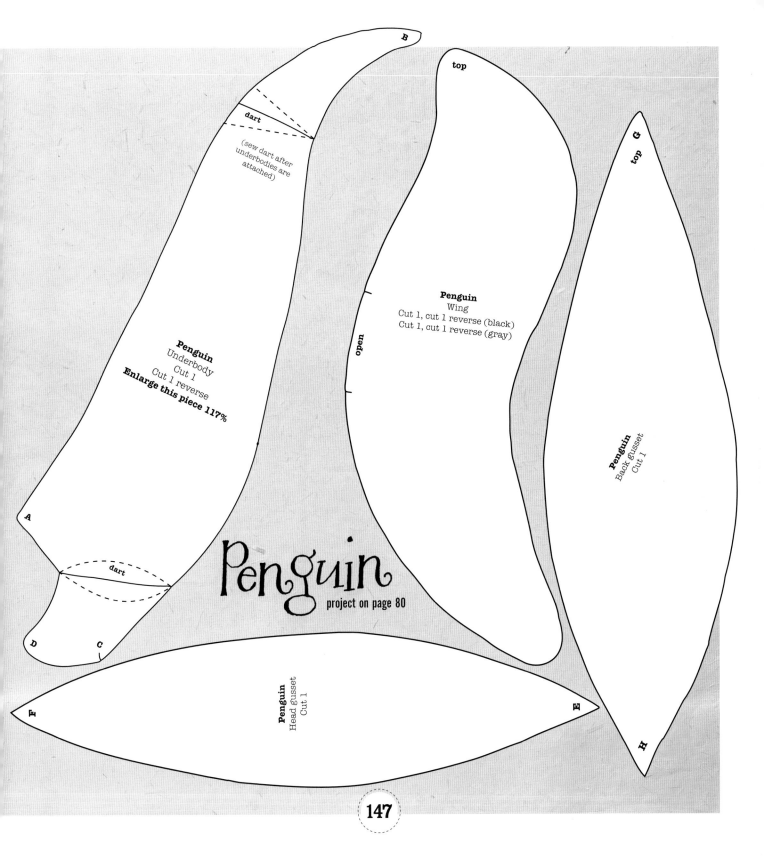

B

dart

(sew dart after underbodies are attached)

top

top

G

Penguin
Wing
Cut 1, cut 1 reverse (black)
Cut 1, cut 1 reverse (gray)

open

Penguin
Underbody
Cut 1
Cut 1 reverse
Enlarge this piece 117%

Penguin
Back gusset
Cut 1

A

dart

D   C

Penguin

project on page 80

Penguin
Head gusset
Cut 1

F

E

H

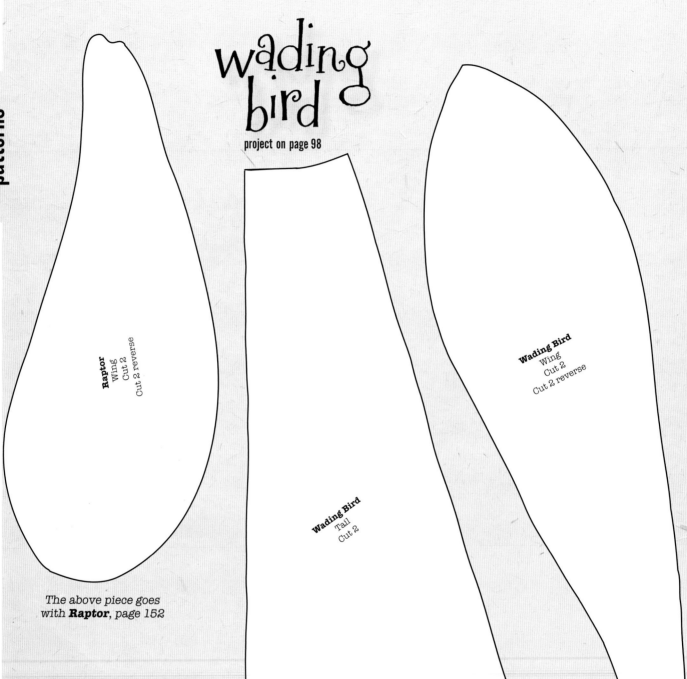

wading bird
project on page 98

Raptor
Wing
Cut 2
Cut 2 reverse

Wading Bird
Wing
Cut 2
Cut 2 reverse

Wading Bird
Tail
Cut 2

The above piece goes
with **Raptor**, page 152

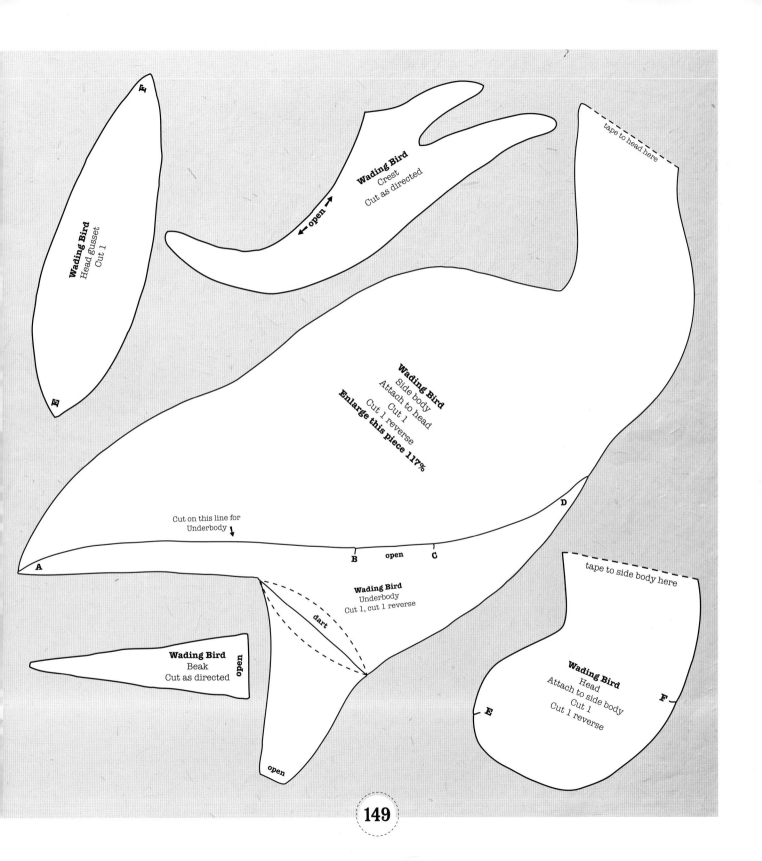

Wading Bird
Head gusset
Cut 1

F

E

Wading Bird
Crest
Cut as directed

← open →

tape to head here

Wading Bird
Side body
Attach to head
Cut 1
Cut 1 reverse
Enlarge this piece 117%

D

Cut on this line for
Underbody ↓

B   open   C

A

Wading Bird
Underbody
Cut 1, cut 1 reverse

dart

Wading Bird
Beak
Cut as directed

open

open

tape to side body here

Wading Bird
Head
Attach to side body
Cut 1
Cut 1 reverse

E

F

E2

E1

Owl
Back gusset
Cut 1
**Enlarge this
piece 117%**

F

Owl
Beak
Cut as
directed

E

B

Owl
Side body
Cut 1
Cut 1 reverse

Owl
Head gusset
Cut 1
**Enlarge this
piece 117%**

F

owl
project on page 86

Cut on this line for
underbody

C

open

A

Owl
Underbody
Cut 1
Cut 1 reverse

D

dart

H ← open → **G**

Owl
Ear
Cut as directed

Owl
Top eye layer
Cut as directed

Owl
Middle eye layer
Cut as directed

open

open

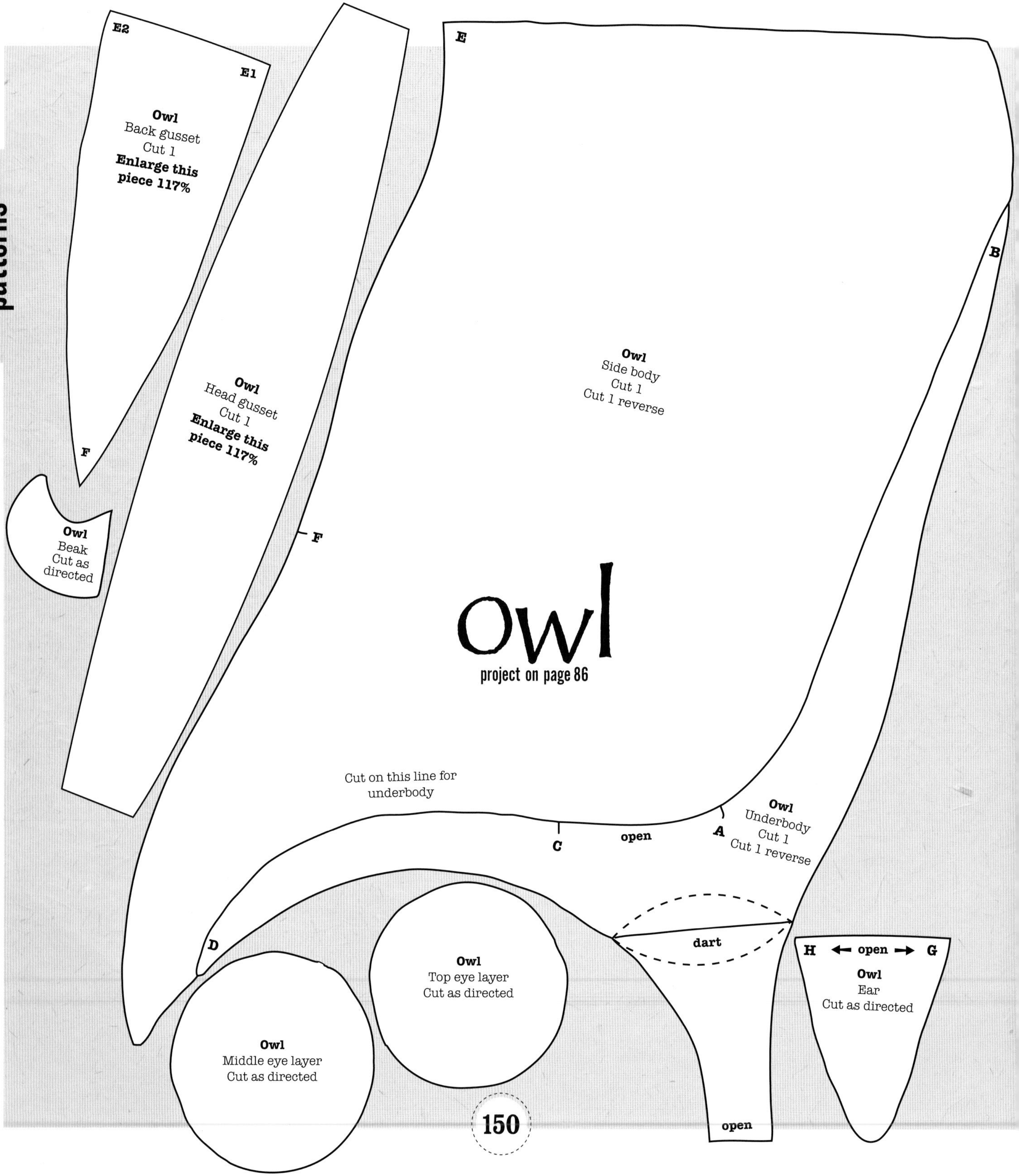

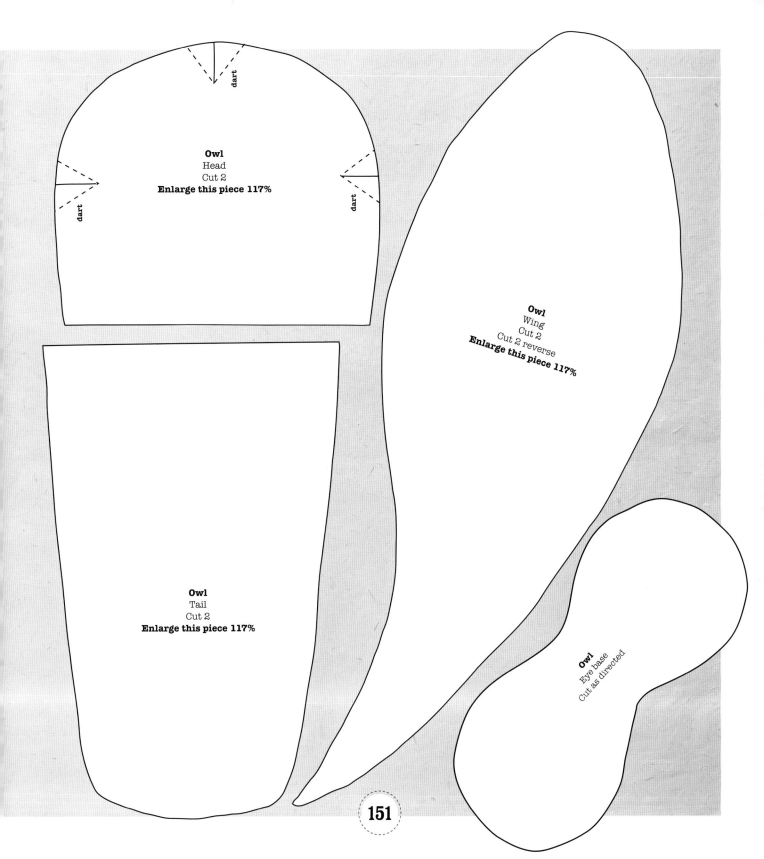

Owl
Head
Cut 2
Enlarge this piece 117%

dart

dart

dart

Owl
Wing
Cut 2
Cut 2 reverse
Enlarge this piece 117%

Owl
Tail
Cut 2
Enlarge this piece 117%

Owl
Eye base
Cut as directed

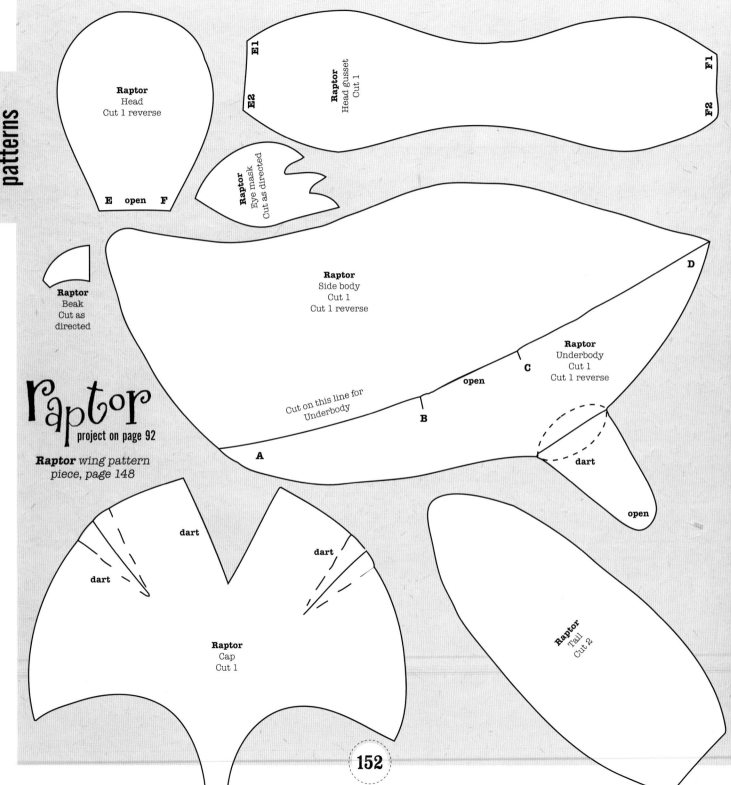

Raptor
Head
Cut 1 reverse

E   open   F

E1

E2

Raptor
Head gusset
Cut 1

F1

F2

Raptor
Eye mask
Cut as directed

Raptor
Beak
Cut as
directed

Raptor
Side body
Cut 1
Cut 1 reverse

D

C

Raptor
Underbody
Cut 1
Cut 1 reverse

open

Cut on this line for
Underbody

B

A

dart

open

raptor
project on page 92

Raptor *wing pattern
piece, page 148*

dart

dart

dart

Raptor
Cap
Cut 1

Raptor
Tail
Cut 2

152

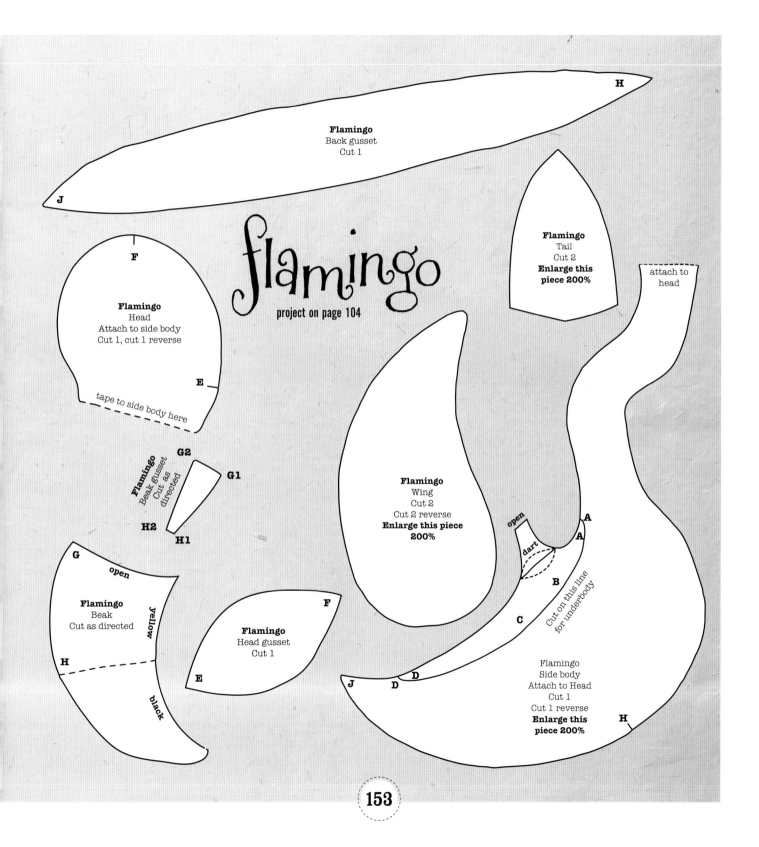

Flamingo
Back gusset
Cut 1

H

J

flamingo
project on page 104

Flamingo
Tail
Cut 2
Enlarge this piece 200%

attach to head

F

Flamingo
Head
Attach to side body
Cut 1, cut 1 reverse

E

tape to side body here

Flamingo
Beak gusset
Cut as directed

G2

G1

H2

H1

Flamingo
Wing
Cut 2
Cut 2 reverse
Enlarge this piece 200%

open

dart

A

A

B

C

Cut on this line
for underbody

G

open

Flamingo
Beak
Cut as directed

Yellow

H

black

Flamingo
Head gusset
Cut 1

F

E

J

D

D

Flamingo
Side body
Attach to Head
Cut 1
Cut 1 reverse
Enlarge this piece 200%

H

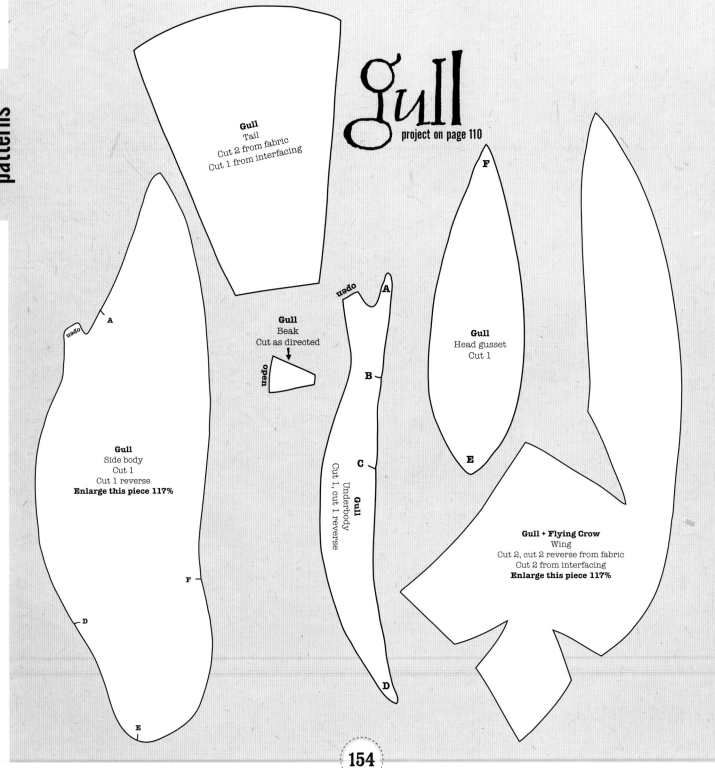

Gull
Tail
Cut 2 from fabric
Cut 1 from interfacing

gull
project on page 110

Gull
Beak
Cut as directed

open

Gull
Side body
Cut 1
Cut 1 reverse
Enlarge this piece 117%

Gull
Underbody
Cut 1, cut 1 reverse

Gull
Head gusset
Cut 1

Gull + Flying Crow
Wing
Cut 2, cut 2 reverse from fabric
Cut 2 from interfacing
Enlarge this piece 117%

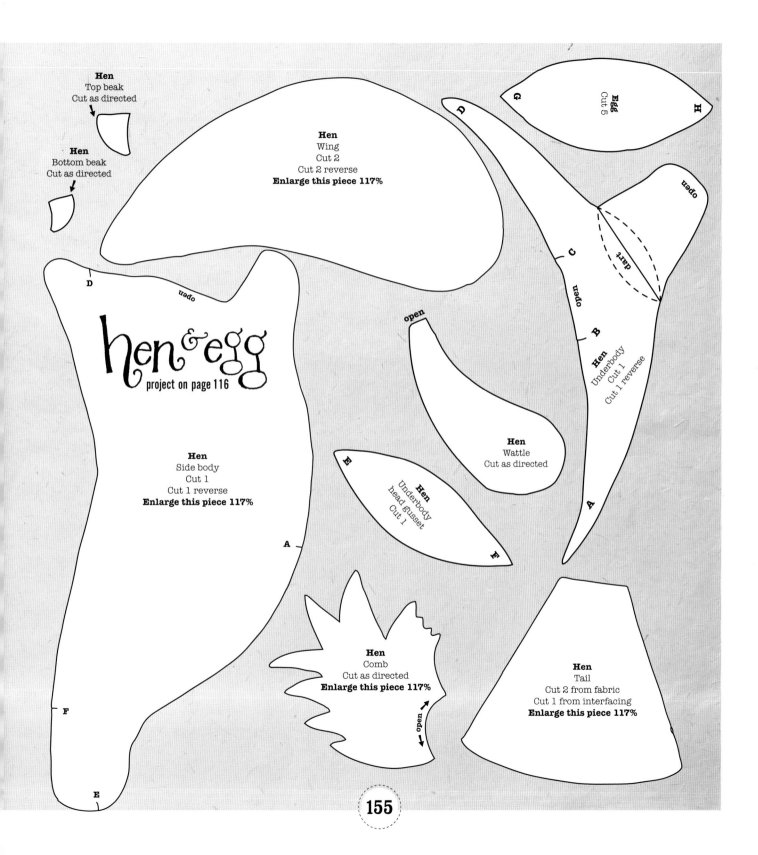

Hen
Top beak
Cut as directed

Hen
Bottom beak
Cut as directed

Hen
Wing
Cut 2
Cut 2 reverse
Enlarge this piece 117%

Egg
Cut 5

G

D

H

open

C

open

dart

B

Hen
Underbody
Cut 1
Cut 1 reverse

A

open

D

open

hen & egg
project on page 116

Hen
Side body
Cut 1
Cut 1 reverse
Enlarge this piece 117%

A

F

E

Hen
Underbody
head gusset
Cut 1

E

F

Hen
Wattle
Cut as directed

Hen
Comb
Cut as directed
Enlarge this piece 117%

open

Hen
Tail
Cut 2 from fabric
Cut 1 from interfacing
Enlarge this piece 117%

peacock
project on page 122

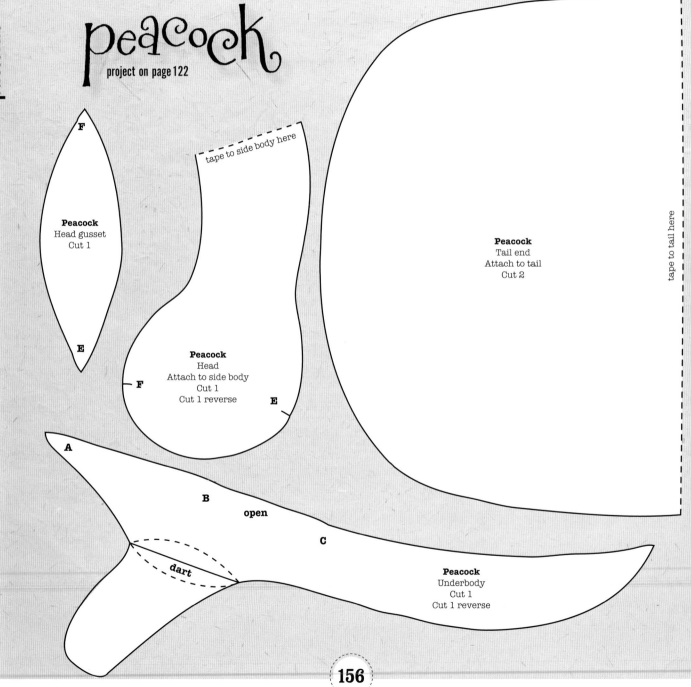

F

tape to side body here

Peacock
Head gusset
Cut 1

E

Peacock
Tail end
Attach to tail
Cut 2

tape to tail here

F

Peacock
Head
Attach to side body
Cut 1
Cut 1 reverse

E

A

B

open

C

dart

Peacock
Underbody
Cut 1
Cut 1 reverse

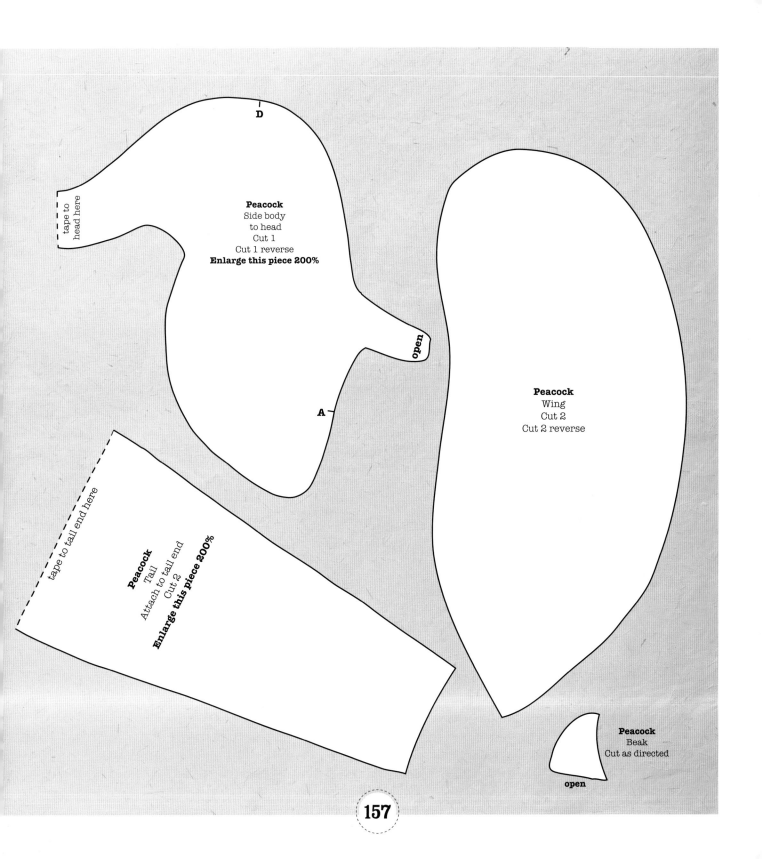

D

Peacock
Side body
to head
Cut 1
Cut 1 reverse
Enlarge this piece 200%

tape to head here

open

A

Peacock
Wing
Cut 2
Cut 2 reverse

tape to tail end here

Peacock
Tail
Attach to tail end
Cut 2
Enlarge this piece 200%

Peacock
Beak
Cut as directed

open

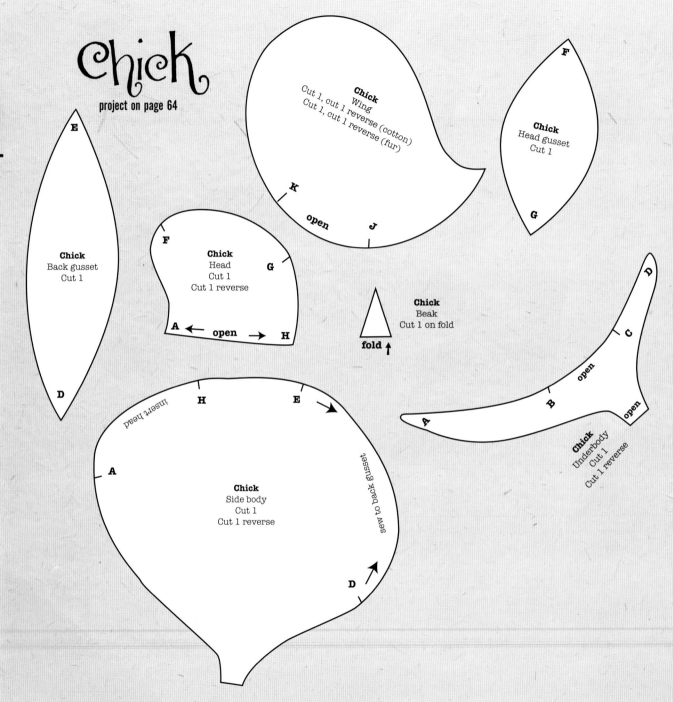

Chick

project on page 64

Chick
Wing
Cut 1, cut 1 reverse (cotton)
Cut 1, cut 1 reverse (fur)

K

open   J

F

Chick
Head gusset
Cut 1

G

E

Chick
Back gusset
Cut 1

D

F   G

Chick
Head
Cut 1
Cut 1 reverse

A   ← open →   H

Chick
Beak
Cut 1 on fold

fold ↑

D

C

open

B   open

A

Chick
Underbody
Cut 1
Cut 1 reverse

insert head

H   E

A

Chick
Side body
Cut 1
Cut 1 reverse

sew to back gusset

D

index

Discover more *creative mixed-media* and *sewing techniques* with these guides from Interweave

Sew Me, Love Me
Best Stuffed
Friends to Make
Hsiu-Lan Kuei
ISBN 978-1-59668-182-8
$19.95

I Love Patchwork
21 Irresistible Zakka
Projects to Sew
Rashida Coleman-Hale
ISBN 978-1-59668-142-2
$24.95

**Stitchy Kitty
Fuzzy Puppy**
60 Motifs to
Stitch Everywhere
Ayako Otsuka
ISBN 978-1-59668-183-5
$19.95

INTERWEAVE
interweave.com